T0283919

on track ...

Daryl Hall & John Oates

every album, every song

Ian Abrahams

sonicbondpublishing.com

Sonicbond Publishing Limited
www.sonicbondpublishing.co.uk
Email: info@sonicbondpublishing.co.uk

First Published in the United Kingdom 2022
First Published in the United States 2022

British Library Cataloguing in Publication Data:
A Catalogue record for this book is available from the British Library

Copyright Ian Abrahams 2022

ISBN 978-1-78952-167-2

Typeset in ITC Garamond & ITC Avant Garde
Printed and bound in England

Graphic design and typesetting: Full Moon Media

on track ...

Daryl Hall & John Oates

every album, every song

Ian Abrahams

SONICBOND

sonicbondpublishing.com

Acknowledgements

Dedicated to my old and much-missed mate David Wilkinson, who himself enjoyed a bit of rock 'n' soul music in our youthful nightclub forays. RIP Wilko.

A shout-out, as always to my own band of musical comrades over the years, including Scott Abraham, Raymond Altree, Joe Beer, Robert Bennetts, Simon Coley, Martin Day, Andrew Dunn, Stuart Miller, Oz Hardwick, Richard Pascoe, Tim Stevens, Keith Topping and Mark Vinson.

Huge thanks to Janet Abrahams for putting up with weekends mostly dedicated to listening to and writing about Daryl Hall and John Oates.

Thanks to Kimberley Healey for that chat about how best to describe the front cover of the 'silver' album in modern language! Many thanks to Joe Cang for his memories of a weekend in Connecticut spent writing and recording with John Oates.

Appreciation to Sean McGhee for the chance to write about Hall & Oates for his R2/RNR magazine a few years back, rekindling my interest in their records. And thanks, of course, to Stephen Lambe and Sonicbond Publishing for the chance to revisit these records again and give them a little love in print.

Foreword

I first encountered the music of Daryl Hall and John Oates right at the height of their 1980s fame, hearing 'I Can't Go For That (No Can Do)' and 'Private Eyes' in the nightclubs of my youth. Because my enthusiasm for music really started with punk rock and new wave, Hall & Oates' music opened my ears to a style I'd not really investigated or embraced previously. I was fortunate in that my local record shop – the much-missed John Oliver's, in Redruth, Cornwall – was the go-to place for extensive back-catalogue vinyl, and so from there, I was able to backtrack through Daryl and John's history (always a treat to discover musicians deep into their career, and uncover those records that make up their legacy and journey) with copies of *Along The Red Ledge*, *Beauty On A Back Street*, *War Babies* and others. From those albums, I could see beyond the caricature that grew up around them in the 1980s and gained a proper understanding of what brought them to my own entry point.

Truth be told, though I loved *Private Eyes* (and still do), and while I was regularly playing most of their earlier catalogue throughout the 1980s, by the time of *Big Bam Boom* and their initial hiatus, I'd started to drift away from them. I enjoyed their first *comeback* album *Ooh Yeah!* a great deal, but my go-to Hall & Oates album was the Japanese CD pressing of *Along The Red Ledge* that I unearthed in Tower Records, Piccadilly in the early 1990s. After that, I lost sight of what they were doing, occasionally converting some of my vinyl editions to CD – foolish as I was in abandoning the format - but letting records such as *Marigold Sky* and *Do It For Love* pass me by.

But I thought about Hall & Oates again when writing for the British music magazine that has variously gone by the names *Rock N Reel*, *R2*, and *RnR* – which contains a back-page column titled 'It Started With A Disc', for which I wrote a piece on my affection for *Along The Red Ledge*: an article I've included in this book's appendices. Following on from that, I was thrilled to do a telephone interview with John Oates on the release of his 2011 solo album *Mississippi Mile*, and really started to think about Hall & Oates' work again in a way I hadn't since their 1980s heyday.

What better way to properly revisit their work and unearth catalogue pieces that had eluded me (most particularly their debut album *Whole Oats*, which proved a frustratingly elusive record in the 1980s, but which is now out there for all to hear) than by tackling their discography via Sonicbond's *On Track* series? It's an opportunity to delve in and get under the skin of this most misunderstood of duos; to consider their smash hits – virtually all distinct in style and tone from each other – and to describe how their more experimental work sat alongside their familiar hits.

So, this book gathers their output, album-by-album, song-by-song, from *Whole Oats* through to their most recent album of principally original material, *Do It For Love*, though I'll also acknowledge the two covers albums they released subsequently. It's a deep dive including notable non-album tracks, demos and a survey of their live and compilation records. But it's not a biography of Daryl Hall and John Oates, and though I'll touch on particular points in their lives, and think about their personal relationship across fifty years, I'm not here to interrogate them as people or to describe their individual life journeys.

Another thing I've decided not to touch on is the modern convention of trying to categorise their music into the clunky and misleading retro-fit genre they call 'yacht rock'. For me, that seems to come from a need to pigeonhole music with hindsight rather than as part of a contemporary movement, and is an entirely invented and unnecessary categorisation that I'm having none of.

One other point is that Daryl and John's records have always been branded as 'Daryl Hall & John Oates' rather than the commonly used moniker 'Hall & Oates': 'We perceive ourselves as being two individuals working together – our joke is that our company is called Two-Headed Monster because that is exactly what we are *not*', as John told me in our interview. Nonetheless, for stylistic variety, I've variously referred to them in the text as Daryl Hall & John Oates, Hall & Oates and 'H&O', even though I'll acknowledge at the outset that the first of those is how they particularly prefer to be known. Ditto in song-publishing credits: I'll name them as 'Hall' and 'Oates', but credit co-writers by full name for clarity.

on track ...
Daryl Hall & John Oates

Contents

Introduction

As first meetings go, it was the stuff of legend: rival gangs slugging it out one night in 1967 at West Philadelphia's Adelphi Ballroom. One of a collection of bands on the bill of that evening's record hop – there to mime to a DJ playing their singles – was The Temptones, featuring one Daryl Hall, at that time possibly still going by his birth name Daryl Hohl. Also on the bill were The Masters, including journalism student John Oates. It's properly kicking off with knives and gunfire, and these two guys are desperate to get the hell out of what's going on. As Daryl recalled:

> We were on the upper floor, and there was a lift down to the street, so I jumped into it, and John Oates was in it too. I said, 'Oh, well, you didn't get to go on either. How ya doin? You go to Temple University. I go to Temple University. See you later'. That's how we met'.

They were very different characters. Gradually gravitating towards each other during their time at Temple, they became friends through a shared love of music, though it would be the start of the 1970s before they started playing music together. Interviewed for a 'how we met' piece for *The Independent*, Hall recalled his future musical comrade as being 'a college wrestler, a sports jock ... I never knew people who did that kind of stuff', and described himself as becoming something of a more worldly-wise mentor to an Oates who – at the peak of peace and love – still had defiantly short hair, though he already sported his soon-to-be-legendary moustache. 'I introduced him to lots of things. 'Take this, smoke that, try this'. I brought him into the world of the late sixties.

In the same interview, Oates reflected on their differences:

> He was very much like me in terms of background, and he liked the same music. On the other hand, he was very different from the other people I knew because he was more forward-looking. He's always had his finger on the pulse of something: everything from hairstyle and the way he dresses to the things he would think about. My nature tends to be more laid-back; he filled in a gap in my personality.

They were working on their individual routes into the music business. Daryl – born in Pottsdown, Pennsylvania, on 11 October 1946 – came from Germanic ancestry and parents who themselves were musical. At Temple University, he majored in music and concurrently worked with The Temptones, and was really a musical gun-for-hire for anyone who called him. The Temptones cut two singles in 1967 – 'Say These Words of Love' b/w 'Something Good' and 'Girl I Love You' b/w 'Good-bye' – with Daryl credited as D. Hohl. He was seventeen and already feeling assured of his talent. Reflecting back, he talked of 'Girl I Love You' as being 'a quintessential early Philly record. Somebody got their name on it, but that was my song. The reason it sounds professional is because the backup people were Gamble and Huff. This was at the beginning of their career as well as mine. We were all starting together in Philadelphia'.

At exactly what point the German lineage of Hohl gave way to Hall, is unclear. But certainly by 1968 – the year after meeting Oates – he's billed on an AMY Records release, as Daryl Hall with the Cellar Door. Hall described it to *Pitchfork*: 'Somebody would say, 'Sing this song' and 'Here's $20', and I would sing whatever song they gave me. There's a horrible record: 'The Princess And The Soldier'. They said, 'Try and sing it like operatic', so I sang it that way. Now this record haunts me and follows me around'.

The following year he cut 'A Lonely Girl' for Parallax Records, receiving a writing and arrangement credit for its B-side 'Vicky – Vicky', but these appear to be the only 1960s single credits under Daryl's name. He'd become one of the session musicians circulating around the Gamble and Huff songwriting/ production team, who themselves were becoming key figures in the Philadelphia soul scene. Both Daryl and John's early singles had appeared on labels backed by Gamble. Hall, still a student by day, considered himself part of their B-team: 'a hanger-outer. But I was around, in the midst of it. I worked with The Stylistics and The Delfonics, the Three Degrees and Jerry Butler, all these people'. The identities behind some of these uncredited contributions – most likely with Daryl providing a varying mix of keyboards and backing vocals – are doubtless lost to history. But, among others, he's known to have played on the Electric Indian novelty record 'Keem-O-Sabe', which he's described as 'one of the stupidest records you ever heard in your life'.

He next appeared, credited again for keyboards and vocals, as part of Gulliver, a band that leaned towards a heavier hippie folk-rock sound than he'd been involved with previously and who released an eponymous LP on Elektra Records in 1970. That album has a number of tracks that have since become familiar to Hall & Oates fans as part of a series of off-catalogue releases badged as Daryl Hall & John Oates (starting with *Past Times Behind*: Chelsea Records, 1976) – compiling various early demos recorded as a duo and separately, alongside some Gulliver tracks – which have since replicated themselves in a myriad of combinations: *A Lot Of Changes Comin'*, *Really Smokin'*, *The Provider*, *First Sessions*... they proliferate.

Talking about those releases, Daryl enthused about a song called 'Perkiomen' that he'd resurrected many years later for his webcast *Live From Daryl's House:* 'I wrote that song when I was twenty. I used to go down to visit John when he lived at his parents' house in New Wales [Pennsylvania]. I had to cross the Perkiomen creek to get there, and the song was inspired by that. It's one of those songs John and I did as a demo. If you ever get that stupid album *Past Times Behind*, it's a series of demos. Some of those songs, John's not even involved in. But out of all that, 'Perkiomen' was on it and I really liked that song'.

John Oates (born 7 April 1948, New York) came from what he described as a 'matriarchal Italian family', and tells how his debut single was cut at the tender age of two in a Coney Island Voice-O-Graph recording booth. In a signpost to the future, he'd return a few years later and record a version of 'All Shook Up' in, he says, that very same booth.

Experimenting with folk music, he developed a lifelong love of rhythm and blues that still informs his solo work. His first proper single was as lead singer and guitarist for The Masters – 'I Need Your Love' b/w 'Not My Baby' – the writing credited to John Oates and Pat Collins:

> The single that Daryl's group did and the single that my group did were very similar to each other in style. They represented what was going on in Philadelphia at that moment in the mid-60s: a kind of Philadelphia R&B style, which of course, I was part of as well. I never did any recordings in my folk days because – and we're talking about the late-1950s/early-1960s – recording was very difficult to do. You had to go to a studio; nobody had tape recorders, so I have no real record of what I was doing in my coffeehouse days, so to speak. Back then, I had two distinct musical personalities; I would be wearing something like a denim work shirt and singing in a coffeehouse doing traditional Appalachian ballads and delta blues, and then the next night, I'd be wearing a Sharkskin suit and playing R&B with a band.

But Philadelphia wasn't enough for John. Once he graduated from Temple, he set out on a journey beyond the USA, landing first in England, travelling by hovercraft across the channel to Calais and onward to Paris, hitching down to Toulouse and catching a train to Barcelona for the Spanish leg of his adventure. Rome, Florence, Lake Como and the Italian Alps later gave way to St. Moritz and then Hamburg, legendary German home of the music scene where The Beatles first made their mark, and even hooking up with a hippie commune in Copenhagen. In his memoir, John recounts how it was a record shop in Amsterdam that made him yearn for his beloved bluegrass music and home, signalling the end of his 1970 European sojourn.

'I busked around Europe for four months', he recalled to *The Guardian* for a piece on his and Daryl's fifty years of friendship. He'd sublet his flat to Hall's sister and her boyfriend, only to discover when he got back that the landlord had changed the locks and he was homeless. 'I had nowhere to go. Daryl [who was married at the time and living in small accommodation] took pity on me and invited me to move in. We were living in this hippie ghetto with a lot of freaks and cool people. All we did was walk around and play music in coffee shops. Little by little, we began to gel and write songs'. From small things like that, too, is the stuff that legends spring from.

The Atlantic Years

Whole Oats (1972)

Personnel:
Daryl Hall: vocals, keyboards, synthesizer, guitar, mandolin, vibraphone, cello
John Oates: vocals, guitar
Bill Keith: pedal steel guitar
Jim Helmer: drums
Arif Mardin: horns
Mike Patto: bass
Jerry Ricks: guitar
Recorded at Atlantic Recording Studios, New York
Producer: Arif Mardin
Release date: 12 November 1972
Label: Atlantic
Chart Placings: US: -, UK: -
Running Time: 38:08

At the start of the 1970s, though they'd been drawn together and Oates moved into Daryl and wife Bryna Lublin's marital home, they were each trying to establish their own musical identity, with the idea of working as a duo being simply one of a number of possible angles. Hall, of course, had Gulliver, which today might be described as a manufactured band, put together as it was by Philly music entrepreneur John Madara (though the effective band leader was singer/songwriter Tim Moore, who also enjoyed the lion's share of the writing credits). Gulliver wouldn't see 1970 out, and though John Oates was recruited into the fold in the band's dying days, he concedes this was only 'briefly as back-up guitar player, and the band broke up pretty quickly thereafter'.

But there's a sense that through 1970 – Gulliver notwithstanding – Daryl and John were starting to see their destinies as being wrapped up in each other. 'We were hippies just scrounging around in Philadelphia', Oates told *Rolling Stone*. 'The whole thing was predicated on, 'Hey man, I've got some songs. You've got some songs. I'm not happy with what I'm doing. You're dissatisfied with what you're doing. Why don't we just do something together and just see what happens?'. It was that casual'. To *Shindig* magazine, he elaborated on how 'Daryl would play a song and I would accompany him. I'd play a song on guitar and he would accompany me on piano. It was two guys who were independent, who just accompanied each other and little by little that became more of a collaboration, and that became more of a sound'.

Though they've both made it clear that their albums should always bear the names Daryl Hall & John Oates – despite a brief introductory foray using the band name Whole Oats – and would disparage its abbreviated Hall & Oates form, the simple starting point was, as Daryl says, that 'we were living in an apartment in Philadelphia, and the mailbox said 'Hall & Oates'. That's how we got the name'. In his memoir, John tells this slightly differently, recalling that while he was still at Temple, he shared an apartment with Hall where the mailbox was labelled as 'Hohl-Oates', therefore being the later inspiration for their initial gigs as Whole Oats. But whatever the timings, as John continues, 'If you look on every album we've ever made, it always has our full names. That was a conscious decision because we felt we were two very different individuals who had a lot in common musically, but who were very different personally'.

Playing as Whole Oats, on 5 December 1970 in the North Philadelphia art gallery Hecate's Circle, they made their debut performance, bar those art gallery and coffee shop pop-ups where they'd started working out their style. This led to repeat appearances there into early-1971, after which they booked studio time to work up their initial ideas and to record covers of songs, such as Doc Watson's 'Deep River Blues', which John describes as 'always one of my favourite songs. It's a classic, and everyone knows it'. Decades later, he based his own song 'Deep River' on it (for his *Mississippi Mile* solo album), 'using the chords, but stretching them out to the new groove'.

Remaining a part of Daryl's early career post-Gulliver, was John Madara, through John Madara Productions, where Hall was on the payroll as a songwriter. In an interview for the website *Forgotten Hits*, Madara recounted how 'Gulliver was not going to be an ongoing act. Daryl really wanted to do his own thing'. Noting that John began sitting in on various sessions with Daryl and his Gulliver bandmate Tom Sellers, Madara said that when Daryl and John started working together, 'I was really blown away by them. The two of them were sensational, writing great songs and performing'. In his extensive interview, Madara claims that Daryl and John – separately and together – cut 'over 40 sides', and positions himself as a key figure in their development through to signing with Atlantic Records: a deal he considers was done behind his back. Madara had a publishing arrangement with Chappell Music, and in 1970, 'took Daryl and John to New York to perform live for Chappell with the sides I'd already recorded with them'.

However, in one of an increasing number of visits to Chappell, they encountered budding impresario Tommy Mottola, who became an ever-present figure as the duo began amassing showcase performances in New York. While they felt that in the hunt for a possible record deal, the wheels were turning slowly under Madara's wing, Mottola seemed enthusiastic and dynamic, even though their contract with Madara was exclusive. In his book *Change Of Seasons: A Memoir*, Oates intimates that the industry feedback they eventually received, was that Madara was driving too hard a bargain for their services. Madara, naturally, had a different view: 'A couple of months went by and I got a call from my attorney saying that they wanted out of their recording contract. Unbeknownst to me, one of their auditions was with Atlantic Records. [Mottola] had told them that he could get them a record deal, but they had to get out of their contract with me first'.

Classic music industry shenanigans one way or another you'd think, but the relationship with Madara irreparably broke down, and Madara settled for some percentage points on their first two Atlantic albums, co-publishing on some of the songs cut during his tenure with the duo, and a continuing interest in reissuing those 40-odd 'sides' cut at the start of their career.

But for Daryl and John, those Madara sessions with their mix of Hall's charming folk and John's clear love of blues and roots fingerpicking provided the blueprint and material that Atlantic, with producer, arranger and company-vice-President Arif Mardin at the helm, could reshape into the debut album *Whole Oats*.

'I'm Sorry' (Hall, Oates)

Though Daryl and John's earliest demos have rebounded on them with notorious regularity, when we get to album one, track one, and compare and contrast against those demos, it's totally clear how those days (of what one commentator succinctly described as 'quivering coffeehouse folk') informed their early official work. 'I'm Sorry' – later covered by Justin Hayward on his post-Moody-Blues 1980 *Night Flight* album – is a great example. It has the ambience and easygoing tone of those early demos, but with a light arrangement that leaves the song room to breathe. Hayward turned it into a steady mid-tempo soft rock number, but the *Whole Oats* version has a charm that repays unearthing this lesser-known corner of the catalogue.

Not that it received due acclaim back in the day. Promotion included a support slot for David Bowie on his US *Ziggy Stardust* tour in autumn 1972, which Oates remembered to *Classic Pop* as being 'where the *bar* is set. At the time, David wasn't a superstar – his management wanted him to be perceived as one. He wouldn't speak to anyone, and we weren't allowed backstage!'. Covering Bowie's gig at Ellis Auditorium, Memphis on 24 September 1972, the reviewer, unimpressed with Bowie, saved even worse ire for the opening act: 'At the least, Bowie's show can objectively be called better than that of his warm-up group Whole Oats: a country-rock quartet. Playing all of their eight numbers in a simple 4/4 time, the group could not even keep the attention of the crowd, which spent much time milling up and down the aisles and tossing several plastic frisbees. One of the Whole Oats' final numbers was titled 'I'm Sorry'. It should have been dedicated to the audience'. Ouch.

'All Our Love' (Hall, Oates)

Still in their folk-rock hippie phase, this won't be the last time they yearn for a life in the country in a bucolic daydream haze. It's an inconsequential and laid-back fantasy of finding 'the good life' far away from the hustle of the city – ironic for a band that went on to embrace city life for the next couple of decades, but they had an initial theme and they were going to stick with it for the moment. It also seems that despite that Bowie support nonsense, Whole Oats were crowd-pleasers, according to an early review praising their 'infectious rock and roll music and good vocal harmony' and describing 'a vitality not found in too many new groups. (They) appear to like what they're doing and are not just going through the motions. Oates' high tenor voice really stands out in the group's harmonies'. We'll assume the reviewer couldn't identify his Hall from his Oates.

'Georgie' (Hall)

I wonder what their 1980s generation of fans – finding Daryl Hall & John Oates through *Voices* or 'Maneater' or *Big Bam Boom* – made of these early songs. 'Georgie' has the gossamer slenderness; the delicate touch, that inhabits most of their early songs: a shock in itself to ears brought up on 'Private Eyes' or 'Out Of Touch'. But it also has a grimness, almost like one of those British shock-to-inform 1970s Public Information Films. Georgie is a young lad, friendly with the country-town Reverend's daughter. They hear the peel of the bell that call's Georgie to his music lesson with the preacher, and they hide down in the nearby river when the Reverend seeks them out. She catches her locket on an underwater branch and drowns. The final verse describes the agonies of the Reverend and his wife after hearing the terrible news.

Whether it's taken from a true story, or a piece of American-gothic fiction, the song has a strong sense of place and character, and lyrically is like nothing else Hall & Oates would go on to do.

'Fall In Philadelphia' (Hall)

Well! For a band that made their name being associated with Philadelphia, their reflection of Philly life at the start of their career is a pretty bleak sketch of poor living conditions, a mugging that happened to John, Daryl's bicycle being stolen, drug sellers on the streets and 'seven million people without a hope'. Perhaps it's Hall's jaunty piano, Arif Mardin's eccentric horn arrangement or the hint of the one day to be legendary Hall and Oates harmonies that simply cause the listener to overlook how downbeat this ode actually is, particularly since it affixes itself to Daryl's urge to move away. Interviewed for the liner notes of an Atlantic H&O collection, Hall claimed to be particularly perplexed by this, saying that though 'the song is about how horrible it is to be in Philadelphia, they still play it there on the radio every fall'.

Introducing the song during a 1991 show, Hall said, 'It's really kind of a depressing song. Certain things have come true in this song. I feel we've gotten much better, believe me. I did move to the country; John moved to the country: prophecy fulfilled. Though we lived in New York for 20 years (laughs). In 1970, everything was true. Anyway, it's a song that isn't true about Philadelphia anymore, *okay*?'. That sense of reparation also came through when he talked about how 'I was looking ahead, not back, and wanted to be international, a man of the world. I never lost sight of who I was and where I came from, and am still so happy that I started there. Everything I do stems from that connection'.

'Waterwheel' (Hall)

This brittle song was summed up best by *Treblezine* as 'Fragile to the point of disintegration; a tender account of a rear-window boyhood that makes as strong an emotional connection as anything they did'. There's a suggestion it was to be the album's third single. It's really hard to hear why – the duo became semi-notorious for their inability to pick the right singles – not because it isn't a great song, it's a gorgeous, heartbreaking and haunting piano ballad. But as a big statement – a calling card – it's not single material. Instead, it's a beautiful song to unearth – one of those tracks that, after it unexpectedly surfaces from the LP, you want to replay and re-examine it. It's astonishing. Don't take my word for it. Axl Rose, telling Daryl and John backstage one night that *Whole Oats* was his favourite H&O album, praised 'Waterwheel' as one of the most beautiful songs he'd ever heard.

'Lazyman' (Hall)

Hall said the following in a 1972 radio session: 'This is about one of our former employers. We used to work for a production company, writing songs in the backroom, and every once in a while, this guy would come in and he'd sit while we were writing, and he'd want his name on the song. He'd make little changes and decide his name should be on it'. No names, no pack drill.

'Goodnight and Goodmorning' (Hall, Oates)

Released as Whole Oats, rather than as Daryl Hall & John Oates, this made a catchy and highly accessible first single – b/w 'All Our Love', establishing a routine they'd generally not deviate from: their B-sides culled from the same album as the A-side song, rather than following the general philosophy of the 1970s that would see artists pick a B-side that would likely be a more experimental piece that hadn't found an album home.

A demo of this song (not released as part of Chelsea Records' 1976 *Past Times Behind* collection, but surfacing since) demonstrates how close their demos were to the final versions: showing the confidence producer Arif Mardin had in the material. Particularly nice on the *Whole Oats* version is Daryl's middle-eight mandolin passage, which gives the track a whole new layer. The vocals and drums, too, are stronger, giving the track presence and definition.

Talking about their early influences in a 'Thirty Years of Hall & Oates' *Billboard* interview, John noted: 'We combined traditional American roots into the Philly sound. There (were) a lot of things going on in the city, like the Philadelphia Folk Festival ... all that folk stuff combined with the R&B is a big part of who we are. I loved Doc Watson, Mississippi John Hurt and all that stuff. When you hear a song like 'Goodnight And Goodmorning' or 'When The Morning Comes' [from *Abandoned Luncheonette*], that's what you're hearing'.

Denny Doherty, of The Mamas & The Papas, cut a version of this song in 1974 for his second solo album *Waiting For A Song*, and Hawaiian pop duo Cecilio

& Kapono recorded it the following year for their album *Elua*, while Graham Bonnet cut an evocative and thoughtful version for his eponymous 1977 album.

'They Needed Each Other' (Hall)
Of the early-1970s demos that emerged as part of *Past Times Behind*, this is the one that made it to *Whole Oats* – its gentle, almost childlike keyboards surviving pretty much intact. Hall's soft-voiced account of two people who care so deeply for each other but become disconnected and grow apart, is underpinned with heartfelt strings mixed sympathetically into the background.

Though *Whole Oats* is almost the forgotten album in the Hall & Oates canon, it clearly gained *some* interest and recognition, with this song also receiving a fairly contemporary cover, with the legendary jazz and musical theatre singer Cleo Laine recording it for her 1974 album *A Beautiful Thing*.

'Southeast City Window' (Oates)
Possessing something of a Paul Simon vibe – very understated and having a country tinge – here are some more wistfully bucolic ruminations. Very lovely, but an example of Daryl and John struggling to position themselves between what Daryl conceded was a 'quiet album' and their attempts to get noticed on the live scene, as he reflected the year after the album's release:

> We've been having a little more difficulty in expressing our music live. We found when we play large halls, it's hard to communicate immediately with people who have never heard our music before. We do a lot of subtle things – ballad type, very quiet, almost like Joni Mitchell/Cat Stevens type stuff. But it's really hard to pull that off in a large hall unless people know who you are, so we've been getting louder and louder.

Asked about playing some of the *Whole Oats* songs from memory today, John was reported to have laughed, and confirmed that 'I could not play 'Thank You For...', but I *could* play 'Southeast', because I had a request for it during my book promo tour. And it shocked me, I thought people had forgotten about it. I relearned it and came up with a better arrangement'.

'Thank You For...' (Oates)
An inconsequential song of a brief romantic encounter, most memorable for its amusing aside where John lists things associated with the colour red (carnations, apples and wine), and then concedes that the wine may actually have been white, 'but I needed the rhyme'. This is one very much stuck in deep-catalogue obscurity; cloying, sweet, and sparse in arrangement. Little surprise that all those years later, John elected to not resurrect it on that book tour. Or was it inspired from a personal moment he'd rather have not revisited?

Never mind, because *Whole Oats* then ends on a song that starts to define the way they'd build on what's good about their debut for their first classic album the following year.

'Lilly (Are You Happy)' (Hall, Oates)

Talking to *Classic Pop*, John described this song as being a moment when 'we started to understand the strengths between our vocal ranges'. Daryl starts to stretch out in the semi-improvisational singing style he'd develop over the coming years, and the famous Hall & Oates harmonies begin to crystallise. It's certainly tempting to see it as both the summation of where they'd arrived at and a hint towards the forward-thinking sound they would refine on *Abandoned Luncheonette*.

The lyric suggests John's observational journalistic eye has sketched the enigmatic Lilly from people watching; possibly someone he thought of as spending her life giving herself to strangers who only take – smiling on the outside and crying inside – and wondering how weary that must make her. It's a poignant and thoughtfully-reflective piece to end their first offering.

Abandoned Luncheonette (1973)

Personnel:
Daryl Hall: vocals, mandolin, electric piano, piano, keyboards
John Oates: vocals, acoustic guitar, wah-wah guitar, electric guitar
Chris Bond: mellotron, electric guitar, acoustic guitar, synthesizer
Hugh McCracken: electric guitar
Steve 'Fontz' Gelfand, Gordon Edwards: bass
Bernard Purdie, Rick Marotta: drums
Ralph MacDonald: percussion
Joe Farrell: oboe, tenor sax, alto sax
Jerry Ricks: acoustic guitar
Pancho Morales: conga
Pat Rebillot: organ
Richard Tee: piano
Gloria Agostini: harp
John Blair: Vi-tar electric violin
Marvin Stamm: flugelhorn
Larry Packer: fiddle
Marc Horowitz: banjo
Hall, Oates, Walter F. Hohl, Katy Mae Hohl, Ronald and Donald Wanner, Christian
Bond, Arif Mardin: Backing vocals
Arrangements: Daryl Hall, John Oates, Chris Bond & Abandoned Band
String and horn arrangements: Arif Mardin
Recorded at Atlantic Recording Studios, New York
Producer: Arif Mardin
Release date: 3 November 1973
Label: Atlantic
Chart Placings: US: 33 (Re-entry 1976)
Running Time: 36:54

Talking in 1973, Hall saw the value of *Whole Oats* as being in 'getting our names around. I'm very happy with the way the album's been received. It's getting good critical talk, good reviews. It's sold well in Philadelphia. It's selling good in New York, the East Coast, and it's doing pretty well on the West Coast too'. But it's also true to think of it as their forgotten album. Collectors' website *Discogs* lists 21 versions of *Whole Oats*, against 58 variants of its follow-up *Abandoned Luncheonette*, and no known pressings outside the US until a British release in 1976. In the US, it slipped out of print until the 1990s, and appearances since have been limited, even when viewed in the context of the continuing erratic availability of most of the duo's 1970s catalogue, whether on Atlantic or their next label RCA.

Oates also saw it as a means to an end, telling Ken Sharp for *Goldmine* in 2020 that it was 'the best we had at that moment. But once we did an album and we had Arif Mardin on our side and a contract with Atlantic Records, and we were on tour, all of a sudden, we had a focus and a point of view. Even though *Whole Oats* was technically our first record, our first real record was *Abandoned Luncheonette*. It was recorded with a purpose which was very distinct and clear'.

That wish to escape the narrow confines of Philadelphia that they'd expressed at various times in the *Whole Oats* lyrics, manifested itself not in a realisation of their bucolic country dreams, but in relocating to New York, where, in John's words, they were 'experiencing the city, and being exposed to a whole new level of musicianship through the goodwill and artistic choices of Arif Mardin and Atlantic. We felt where we needed to be. We had high hopes'. It put them at the centre of things, with a producer who could harness them in a sympathetic way, and saw them working with some of the day's leading session players – like drummer Bernard Purdie (famous for his 'Purdie shuffle' and for being Aretha Franklin's musical director) and Hugh McCracken: session guitarist *par excellence* – and called up by Van Morrison, Paul McCartney and Aretha among others: a massive step forward. To then be at Atlantic Studios rubbing shoulders with Aretha, Bob Dylan and Led Zeppelin, their self-declared high hopes must've seemed justified beyond their wildest dreams.

Most critical to their maturing as musicians was their relationship with Arif Mardin – someone they came to see as a mentor, and whose identification of their potential was the key to their Atlantic signing. 'We had auditioned for many, many labels when we were just starting out, and we had a lot of interest, but no one seemed to want to sign us', said John. 'We eventually auditioned at Atlantic and Arif just turned around to the business guys and said, 'I want to produce these guys'. His endorsement was all they needed to know'.

Once again sharing an apartment, Daryl and John were at this point playing with a five-piece Whole Oats band and promoting their debut LP with what must've been very challenging fish-out-of-water support slots for acts as diverse as comedy duo Cheech & Chong and on the aforementioned David Bowie tour. But they'd gathered all the components for a good shot at a second album that would undoubtedly move them up a notch. They were adding to the group of people coalescing around them, which included guitarist and keyboard player Christopher Bond. As both a live and studio musician, and then as co-producer in the mid-1970s, Bond would have quite a push and pull influence on their sound. Even more critically, with Hall's marriage to Bryna dissolving during 1972, both Daryl as an individual, and Daryl Hall & John Oates as songwriters and musicians, would be changed by the arrival of Sara 'Sandy' Allen, as songs on their next two albums would describe.

Sessions for *Abandoned Luncheonette* began early in 1973. John notes them in his memoir as commencing in April but then goes on to talk about Session #4 and the recording of 'She's Gone' as being on 3 March and though he's often said the album was written over the previous year, he's mentioned 'Lady Rain' as being one of the early-1971 demos. There's no evidence to confirm this, however, and it could simply be a title that got reused for a newer song.

But something was really starting to work: from the growing confidence in the writing to the perfect arrangements that Mardin coaxed from those songs. '[He] carefully crafted each song', said Oates, 'every bit of nuance, bringing in the perfect players for the right moments. And it all worked together as one beautiful tapestry'.

'When The Morning Comes' (Hall)
Immediately it's clear that instead of deviating from the folk-soul style of *Whole Oats*, they're building on those early demos that led to that album: almost in a once-to-do-it, once-again-to-do-it-right approach, with Arif Mardin now much more influential and hands-on with arrangements. Where *Whole Oats* tracks had been understated and spruced up from the demos without deviating too far from their source, this dual acoustic opener is rich in sound. It was a huge step forward – a gorgeous realisation of a bittersweet listlessness counterpointed against the easygoing optimism of simply accepting that 'It'll be alright, when the morning comes'. Hall reaches for his falsetto, and towards the end, Christopher Bond comes in with some Mellotron for added texture. As the LP's second single, it faded without trace, but as the album opener, it was a clear signal of how far they'd already come.

'Had I Known You Better Then' (Oates)
Hall picked this as an Oates song he wishes he'd written, describing it as 'a fantastic song ... a particularly great song'. Their voices – Oates in his baritone and Hall in the higher register – combine so well here, with offset words and the embellishment of a lead-guitar motif. John's rumination on a girl's face fleetingly glimpsed becomes a charming daydream set down in music. John described to me:

Everyone says that it's such a sweet love song and that it must've been based on a poignant, emotional experience, and yet really what it was, was that I was standing on a street corner in Philadelphia, and this bus pulled up in front of me, and out of this dirty window this girl was looking at me and I was looking at her and it was in the moment, and the bus pulled by and I wrote that song. Songwriters are like inspirational vampires: we have to take it when we can get it!

'Las Vegas Turnaround (The Stewardess Song)' (Oates)
One of the best-loved Oates songs not to have been released as a single, and still a staple live favourite, this fleet-footed charmer came from a conversation John had with a couple of stewardesses who informed him they were on a 'Las Vegas turnaround'.

I'd never heard that term before. They said, 'That's when we take a bunch of gambling fools to Las Vegas and back'. My songwriting antenna went up and I

23

thought, 'That's a really cool thing to build a song around'. One of these girls turned out to be Sara, who eventually became Daryl's girlfriend.

Hall met Sara 'Sandy' Allen after the breakup of his first marriage, while she was an air stewardess for Capital Air. Described as his constant companion, indeed they maintained a relationship for the best part of thirty years, the elusive Allen was captured in words by the magazine *Circus* in 1977, via a simple description of her as 'a Lauren Bacall-style beauty'.

'She's Gone' (Hall, Oates)
Though when first released as a single, this perennial classic managed only regional hit status, in, naturally, Philadelphia, reaching No. 60 as their first US-charting 7". It would go on to become top ten when reissued in 1976, off the back of 'Sara Smile', from the eponymous 'silver' album, with Atlantic Records cashing in on the success Daryl and John would start to enjoy after moving to RCA. Though sometimes associated with the failure of Daryl and Bryna's marriage, John recounted the more-often-told story of 'She's Gone' to *The Independent*:

(It was) about a girl I met in Greenwich Village in the middle of the night, wearing a tutu and cowboy boots. We'd seen each other once or twice and arranged to meet for New Year's Eve. But she didn't show up, so I sat on my own with this acoustic guitar, playing this sorrowful lament. It was quite a folky old refrain. When Daryl came in the next day, he sat down at the piano and gave it a more groove-orientated R 'N' B sound.

Again, those fans who discovered the duo in the 1980s might be surprised at the dynamic here, with this being very much John's song in the vocal, where later, for something such as 'Out Of Touch' – similarly an Oates song developed with a Hall co-write – the natural thing was for Daryl to assume the lead role and John to be much more in the background. That chimes with how Daryl described the next years, in a feature on *Abandoned Luncheonette* for *American Songwriter*: 'We were really clicking as a creative team in those days. There are a lot of great John Oates moments on that album that still really impress me. Things sort of evolved after that. I took on more, and the balance shifted of what our functions were. But in those days, we were just kids and we were just trying'.

We can't leave 'She's Gone' without touching on the quite bizarre promotional film, now preserved forever in public on the likes of YouTube, and in its way just as peculiar as the image of the anonymous Greenwich Village girl in the tutu and cowboy boots. Starting with a grainy image of the abandoned luncheonette, it fades in via green-screen effects, to Daryl and John, seated separately: John in bow tie and bib, Daryl in a black bathrobe, black socks and white three-strap sandals, a nobody needs to see this image, all told. John lip-synchs the verse while Daryl vaguely does the same in the chorus as Sandy Allen strides across the front of the screen in a floral dress. Disinterest etched on his face, Daryl takes a drag on a cigarette as John mimes the second verse and continues to do so even in the moments where he should be pretending to deliver the high notes. Sara walks back again, followed by their tour manager dressed in a Devil outfit. More wafting across the stage by Sara and the Devil, and then John is helped into a *penguin* suit with flippers for hands, before he takes the guitar lead into the final chorus. They'd make some strange videos in the 1980s for the MTV generation, but nothing matches this psychedelic trip.

Shot by his film-student sister, John described it to *Yahoo Entertainment* as 'performance art', recalling it as being a promotional solution they came up with to avoid lip-synching on an Atlantic City dance show:

I said, 'Let's do something crazy'. Here's this 20-year-old girl with a script we had all written together ... she walks into the control room and starts telling these guys what we're doing. We did the video and they hit the ceiling. They thought we were mocking them. They did not play the video on the show, and they called our record company and said they would never play us again! And we were laughing all the way!

'I'm Just A Kid (Don't Make Me Feel Like A Man)' (Oates)
In his book *Change Of Seasons: A Memoir*, Oates described this angst-ridden acoustic coming-of-age number as being conceived during an evening spent in the audience of New Jersey's Capitol Theatre, where he looked around and – even being in his early-20s – saw that so many of the audience were a lot younger than him. But there's also a sense in this song that if that observational experience was the springboard, the song expanded to become a rumination on being on the cusp of life's experiences and not wanting to be pushed into maturity too soon. Lyrically it's a bit clumsy and unrefined ('will you survive/learn to drive' sounds like rhyming desperation, even if it's a metaphor, perhaps, for taking sexual control, doesn't it?) and the years haven't really been too kind to its 'Little girl what's your name' opening line and its characterisation of the 'cradle thief'. Honestly, the passage of time has just made some of this one seem a bit off. It happens.

'Abandoned Luncheonette' (Hall)
Now, this is a *bona fide* classic album cut and no mistake. Hall has on occasion expressed dissatisfaction with side two – which this opens – suggesting that Christopher Bond was leading the music down a route influenced by his own love of The Beatles, which Daryl professes to have not particularly shared in those days. But this song is a glorious haze of longing, reflection and regret. Full of clever effects and satisfying texture changes taking the narrative backwards and forward in time, it's almost several different songs in

one, expertly marshalled by Arif Mardin's arrangement, which creates a filmic experience in its realisation of lives slipping by unnoticed.

For Daryl, the luncheonette was part of the fabric of his life: the Rosedale Diner, abandoned in Pottstown, Pennsylvania, near his grandmother's home. He told *American Songwriter*: 'It's a song that could have been called 'Abandoned Lives'. It's about people who gave up and wound up in the same place they started in, only not as good'.

'Lady Rain' (Hall, Oates)

This features the intriguingly-named Lady Vi-tar – an instrument created by Lars Erickson, played and adapted by lesser-known jazz musician John Ellington Blair using an enhanced pick-up (described in his obituary as being a six-stringed combo violin, viola and guitar). Blair had appeared on Alice Coltrane's 1971 album *Universal Consciousness*. The instrument creates an eldritch background soundscape behind the instrumental break – not quite jazz, not exactly progressive; a curious diversion from an already lightly experimental track. Perhaps it was that Beatles thing Hall heard Chris Bond bring to the sessions, though by the time they played it on UK music show *The Old Grey Whistle Test* in 1976, extended lead guitar and a judicious bit of synthesizer filled the places in the song where the Vi-tar had originally made its mark, making it an altogether more rock-orientated version.

John told the *Something Else* webzine: 'There's something about *Abandoned Luncheonette* that captures the spirit of when (we) first bonded. Even in my solo shows, I do a lot of its songs. I bring out 'Lady Rain' and other things like that. It's one of those records that has stood the test of time'.

'Laughing Boy' (Hall)

Daryl and a piano, and a lyric that's in keeping with the passing of time and the fading of dreams that he'd written about in 'Abandoned Luncheonette'. But this has the twist that while the diner characters were clearly defined and crafted in an observational way, the character here might well be the singer himself. If so, the admonishment of being the friend that knows the protagonist's laugh is a lie becomes a churned-up, angst-ridden internal monologue. Whether that or simply a sketch of someone who once had everything – the magic touch – and lost himself along the way, it's a downbeat, introverted, sober piece that only seems more so when Marvin Stam's flugelhorn arrives to accentuate its mournful demeanour.

'Everytime I Look At You' (Hall)

Oates felt this song summed up what had gone before on the album, though it adds a funky improvised outro and seems to signal a change of direction: which there would be, just not in this style. It's a stretched-out, confident end and quite joyous in its wild hillbilly jam coda to what's really their first proper album – as Oates contested, an album with 'focus and direction, and a group of songs that were very coherent in our eclectic way'.

Talking to *Record Collector*, Daryl noted how this album was the point where their partnership really coalesced: 'We were getting serious as an act. I was still doing demos with other artists and I was still a gun for hire. But those were jobs; this was me. Arif encouraged a more ambitious sound that defined us'.

War Babies (1974)

Personnel:
Daryl Hall: vocals, keyboards, synthesizer, guitar, mandolin, vibraphone
John Oates: vocals, keyboards, synthesizer, guitar
Todd Rundgren: lead guitar, backing vocals
Richie Cerniglia: lead guitar on 'Is It A Star'
John Siegler: bass
John 'Willie' Wilcox: drums
Hello People, Gail Boggs, Sara Allen (Credited as Sandy Allen)
Recorded at Secret Sound Studios, New York
Producer: Todd Rundgren
Release date: 19 October 1974
Label: Atlantic
Chart Placings: US: 86, UK: -
Running Time: 43:25

If *Abandoned Luncheonette* ticked a lot of boxes in refining the sound that Daryl and John were working towards, through their 'sides' cut with John Madara and the lessons they'd learned from working with Arif Mardin in capturing that early potential and really making something special from it, that didn't translate into sales, and the record failed to reach the *Billboard* album chart. With the two accompanying singles achieved only a solitary showing at No. 60 for 'She's Gone', while 'When The Morning Comes' disappeared without a trace, proud as they were of the album, it must have seemed as though commercial success was as elusive as ever.

They continued to work hard as a live act, now finding themselves on more sympathetic bills, sharing a November 1973 residency with Bruce Springsteen at Max's Kansas City in New York, and appearing alongside him in *Record World*'s list of rising stars for that year. Springsteen's biographer Christopher Sandford describes The Boss at the time as playing to overflowing houses at Max's then, but also being, in the words of the great journalist Lester Bangs, 'raved-about and totally broke', and that cold financial reality probably also applied to Hall & Oates on that week-long bill.

Remember, though, how they'd bemoaned the difficulties in translating their light folk-rock and soulful pop into a venue-filling sound? They were about to take a completely new approach for their 'difficult' third album, riding the coattails of progressive rock and seemingly about to, well, abandon the sound of *Abandoned Luncheonette* completely. Their partner-in-crime for this abrupt change of direction was producer Todd Rundgren, an acquaintance of Hall's back in Philadelphia, who'd since found success, first with psychedelic rockers Nazz, and then as a solo artist, though his own *volte-face* album – 1973's *A Wizard, A True Star* – hit similar commercial buffers to those Daryl and John were experiencing. Hall explained to *Clash* magazine: 'We were contemporaries. He wanted to go against the grain and do a whole Beatles

kind of thing in the midst of Philadelphia music. He had all these different
bands. He was trying *not* to be Philadelphia. He left a year before I did, to go to
New York'.

That scattergun approach had seen Rundgren advance far beyond Daryl's
success at that point. At the time of producing *War Babies*, Rundgren had
formed the notable prog-rock band Utopia, but he was already on the path that
would also make his name in production. He'd partially produced Badfinger's
1971 record *Straight Up*, Ron and Russell Mael's pre-Sparks eponymous
Halfnelson LP, New York Dolls' self-titled debut, and a pair of recordings for
Grand Funk Railroad. For the Dolls, and through sessions described as having
creative conflicts, Rundgren had received plaudits from the band for capturing
their live sound in the studio. Conversely, with Hall & Oates, his mission was to
record the duo how they *wished* they sounded in concert. 'As soon as I moved
to New York, we did start travelling in the same circles. I thought it was logical
for him to work with us, because of our different-but-the-same backgrounds',
Daryl recalled.

The result appeared to be a car crash at the time. But the passing of years
(and a similar lack of continuous availability such as *Whole Oats* suffered
from) has given the album space to breathe and has brought a modern
appreciation that was conspicuously absent upon its release. Members of
Rundgren's Utopia were the backing band for the sessions, causing listeners
to hear the results as more of a Utopia spin-off than a Daryl Hall & John Oates
album, while Oates is strangely missing from many of the writing credits,
causing others to unfairly claim this as a Daryl Hall solo album in all but name.
Rundgren told his biographer Paul Myers: 'I think there was this sense at
the label that I was supposed to steer them into something a little more like
SOMETHING/ANYTHING. I was thrown under the bus by the manager at the
time and blamed for all of it'. Daryl, who has continued a close friendship
with Rundgren ever since, has been described as 'bristling' at any suggestion
the *War Babies* production was to blame for it being declaimed as their least
commercial album.

In 1998, John summed up the Atlantic years for *Spin* magazine, characterising
those three albums as 'a dump album, a smart one with *Abandoned
Luncheonette*, and a fucking weird hard-rock one with *War Babies*, which got
us dropped in favour of the Average White Band'. Contemporary reviews of the
weird one were not kind. Namechecking 'She's Gone', *Rolling Stone* lamented
the loss of 'the sweet solo and the two-part singing, full-bodied arrangements
and unblushingly sentimental songs', and raged that 'It's extremely rare for
still-growing artists to show this disdain for the audience they've managed to
win'. *Creem*'s reviewer claimed, '*War Babies* wouldn't really interest me if it
weren't so dominated by Todd', crediting 'the true star' as bringing 'some of
those nifty riffs and syncopations' to proceedings as though they were 'a shot
in the ass'. In the UK, the *NME* was kinder, but again focused on the Rundgren
angle: 'To be fair, his control-panel work is invariably the best around, whether

its upbeat rhythm or straight-ahead melody, both of which the album has
in abundance', hoping against hope that 'having worked on it will rescue
Rundgren from the Utopia he's unfortunately ensconced in'. Good reviews,
bad reviews, they all laid themselves at Todd Rundgren's door. Whose record
was this again?

'Can't Stop The Music (He Played It Much Too Long)' (Oates)

Oates' only solo writing credit here is the tale of a musician who's reached
the heights of success and ended up jaded and disillusioned, setting the
scene for a concept album, given that half of the *War Babies* songs utilise that
theme of creative burnout. *Creem*'s Robert Duncan – whose consideration
of Rundgren's role reads as though Hall and Oates were bit players on their
own record – thought they'd taken this idea to excess: 'As some sort of
sociological metaphor, it's a bit overused ... as a commentary on the music
business, it becomes totally unnecessary. These guys haven't seen the half of
it, 'cause they ain't stars'. This wasn't the album that would make them stars
either, but the track is a lush start with its chiming guitar intro and soft rock
production: much more dense than any of Arif Mardin's work with them. It's
a pretty infectious and catchy song, benefiting from layered production and
transcending its bleak subject matter while holding onto something of the
Philly sound they'd started with.

'Is It A Star' (Hall, Oates)

Asked by the *New York Post* to pick one H&O song that summed up his life,
Oates picked 'Is It A Star', saying 'It represents something that I was going
through as a person in their 20s ... wondering why all this was happening
to me and whether people liked me for who I really was'. With a signature
Rundgren segue in from 'Can't Stop The Music...', it picks up on that song's
sentiments, asking whether it's the actual person on stage or simply the
star aura that the fan sees – that disconnect between the fan's view of the
object of their fandom, and the reality of what's happening inside the mind
of the musician they're so devoted to. One of the early songs that have been
resurrected for their modern live set, 'Is It A Star' is a fan favourite that's stood
the test of time.

'Beanie G And The Rose Tattoo' (Hall)

In a sense, this is an experimental work that eases itself in. Production aside,
the prior songs have some sort of lineage from the earlier albums, but, as Max
Bell identified in his review for the *NME*, 'While 'Can't Stop The Music' and
'Is It A Star' work on their own terms, 'Beanie G And The Rose Tattoo' has
Todd's scorching electric guitar ripping it up ... Despite influences, Rundgren's
production is far closer to the East Coast punch associated with Steely Dan and
The Rascals than the ersatz stodge perpetrated by the Philly Sound'.

This is where *War Babies* really parts company with what we've heard before; where it becomes a Daryl Hall experimental record – Hall always the one most likely to push boundaries anyway – or a Daryl and Todd work. It's no surprise that in the future, Hall and Rundgren would take the opportunity to dust this one off if they were playing together. Simply put, the song has nothing in common with earlier work – It's a swirling cacophony of lead guitar lines and psychedelic stylings. In a fascinating analysis on the *Todd Rundgren Connection* blog in 2003, Jeff Gauss describes the track's 'stinky funk synth sounds', and hears it 'screaming P-Funk through a slightly whitened Philly filter'.

'You're Much Too Soon' (Hall)

Curiously, this cautionary tale of a relationship where one person quickly becomes much more intense than the other comes early in Daryl and Sara Allen's long-term partnership, which may, of course, be pure coincidence, but it's clearly self-aware in some sense, with Hall claiming, 'Don't think I'm blown away by what I am/It's just a job that keeps me travelling'. In that respect, it links back to the 'Is It A Star' description of the disparity between stage persona and offstage reality.

'70's Scenario' (Hall)

Pausing just a moment to note that the title is grammatically wrong, this is often heard as the 1960s coming down with a bump. Here is the crash of the album's titular baby boomer generation: a youthful flourish that revealed the absence of the pot of gold at the end of the rainbow that the decade's newfound freedom had promised. *NME*'s Max Bell wrote of this song: 'When they try and be socially telling, it doesn't quite come off'. Actually, though it tries to be a little too clever, the song's first half is affecting and melancholy, with Hall's vocal particularly powerful. But when Rundgren's spiky lead guitar arrives, it loses its way.

'War Baby Son Of Zorro' (Hall)

Claiming this as to be the album's centrepiece, Rundgren told his biographer Paul Myers that by this point in the album, it's all about the 'high-concept music' and done with 'no intention of making anything resembling a pop song'. Mission accomplished, Todd. There's something of David Bowie about this Cold War survey, which opens with an air-raid siren, capturing the atomic-age nuclear bomb obsession, hiding under desks at the three-minute warning drill, moving on to the impact of Vietnam, while evoking bygone anti-heroes and villains: Zorro – pulp writer Johnston McCulley's 1919 creation – the O.K. Corral's legendary lawman Wyatt Earp, and the more contemporary machinations of Joseph McCarthy. Gunshots ricochet and TV broadcast sounds emerge from static noise, while dense piano duels with acute lead guitar. Sara Allen pops up on backing vocals, Tommy Mottola apparently adds some modulated speech, and it's just entirely mad.

'I'm Watching You (A Mutant Romance)' (Hall)

This character piece, built on sparse noir-ish piano and whispered vocals, recounts watching a prostitute as she pitches up, regular as clockwork, near 42nd and 8th, making her observer think back to a girl he longed for in high school – to the point that when a punter arrives, it hits him just as though he was right back there seeing that unrequited love pair off with another boy. He knows the prostitute is aware she's being watched all night long, but he also knows she believes he'll never make his move because 'You think of me as a steel machine'. It's a sharp piece of writing.

'Better Watch Your Back' (Hall)

This is an odd one – a fussy mid-tempo rocker with hints of calypso and psychedelia, diverting into a hazy shimmer at points, punctuated in a similar way to 'Abandoned Luncheonette'. But instead of signalling a time transition, it seems to represent a moment of lucidity in the life of the central character – described as a 'mad man', who certainly comes across as violent and opinionated – with acute lead guitar highlighting the relentlessness that drives him onwards into trouble, to the despair of his wife. It's another well-sketched piece, with a sense of small-town claustrophobia and a proper air of menace.

'Screaming Through December' (Hall)

Now they've arrived at prog, or at least the American version of prog: overwritten, overly long, overwrought and too clever by far. At one point, it mires itself in sirens and aural effects that sound like Doctor Who's TARDIS trying to materialise, then thinks about making a funky instrumental break, before it drops into free-form jazz with portentous voice-overs and declamations of 'Quasar! Quasar!'. Then we're back to the album's predominant theme of touring burnout and self-destruction, with Faustus – already destroyed from the rigours of playing too many Jersey bars – seemingly reaching his end when he 'ate glass for an appetizer'. Six and half minutes of this. Really.

'Johnny Gore And The 'C' Eaters' (Hall, Oates)

Legend has it that this title came from driving past a marquee sign for a concert by Johnny Gore & The Cheaters, where the 'h' in 'Cheaters' had vanished. Ironically, that band had released a country album titled *I Won't Be A Cheater Anymore*, though the H&O titular derivation is perhaps an apocryphal story since that record came out in 1971, and there's little trace of Gore afterwards. It might just as likely be that someone at the *War Babies* sessions knew the record and judiciously adapted the title.

It's certainly a closing track like no other in their catalogue – a raucous rock 'n' roll brew with a definite nod to 'Johnny B. Goode' (lyrically), metal, glam rock and proto-punk. John saw it as reflecting their move to New York: 'We could feel the chaos and whole vibe and speed of New York, and it started to infuse where we were coming from. We started writing all these weird songs about being on the road – songs like 'Johnny Gore And The 'C' Eaters', because we wanted to rock. Todd helped facilitate that'.

Daryl noted in a 2019 *Record Collector* interview how he'd 'listened to that album recently. It's so ridiculous, it makes me laugh. But it is incomparable and free-spirited, an outside mood as raucous as the environment in which it was made. I got that out of my system. It was chaotic'. More people would argue that Rundgren *dominated* it rather than facilitated it, with reviewers then and now more likely to hold the view that *War Babies* was a Rundgren LP with Daryl and John glued onto it in varying degrees of discomfort. Which isn't to say it's not a good album; viewed outside the H&O canon, it has a prescience and bravery that makes it well worth rediscovering since it has a reputation that's a deterrent to exploring its eclecticism, coupled with being another part of their 1970s catalogue that hasn't been served terribly well with reissues and availability. You know what? Play it loud; there's a lot to like.

Related tracks
Atlantic Records released the first H&O compilation *No Goodbyes*, in February 1977. It came hot on the heels of achieving a retrospective *Billboard* top ten hit with 'She's Gone' the previous year – itself riding on the success of 'Sara Smile': culled from their first RCA album *Daryl Hall & John Oates*. *No Goodbyes* ('An album that never really was; a non-album', according to Daryl: 'A greatest non-hits that Atlantic put out when John and I had left the label back in the mid-70s') featured tracks from all three Atlantic-era LPs, plus a trio of previously unreleased songs.

'Love You Like A Brother' (Hall, Oates)
The three new *No Goodbyes* songs are all Arif Mardin productions that appear to have been recorded after the Todd Rundgren *War Babies* sessions and cut with this compilation in mind. John suggested in his memoir that they were essentially agreed upon as an unlocking of the Atlantic contract: a quid pro quo for releasing the duo to RCA. That indicates that *No Goodbyes* wasn't – as some have suggested – simply an opportunistic cash-in on the duo's growing success, as some have suggested. But the song seems to have more in common with the early demos of *Past Times Behind*. It's a tale of lost love – a treacherous transfer of affection to the narrator's best friend – and a group of three pals now torn apart by it, that's underdeveloped and doesn't quite flow despite having more than the germ of a good idea.

'It's Uncanny' (Hall)
Issued as the *No Goodbyes* single, and no doubt a disappointment by being nowhere near the hit Atlantic had enjoyed with 'She's Gone', this song emerged the year before on a single by the little-known Ray Crumley, credited to writers John Hall and Daryl Oates. Perhaps despite that error, Crumley was

a fan and had heard this song at a 1973 concert, as it appears as the opener on the setlist for an 18 November show at Hempstead, NY, on the *Abandoned Luncheonette* tour. It was also likely, as was perhaps the case with other early H&O covers, such as the Cleo Laine recording, that Chappell Music had a keen eye, or even a fallback plan, on promoting the duo as writing talent for others.

'I Want To Know You For A Long Time' (Hall)

This would've been a much better single than 'It's Uncanny'. From the Martini-advert sweep of its orchestration to the soulful Hall vocals, it is sumptuous and glossy, and pointed to the style they'd find over the first RCA albums. As a signing-off from their partnership with Arif Mardin, it encapsulates how much they'd learned from him. When Mardin died in 2006, his obituaries talked of his twelve Grammys, his arrangement work on Dusty Springfield's *Dusty In Memphis* and his falsetto regeneration of The Bee Gees career. But they also talked about his prominence in the creation of blue-eyed soul, and 'the sophisticated mainstream style of rhythm and blues made by white musicians that he developed, working with artists like Daryl Hall and John Oates'.

RCA Years Part One
Daryl Hall & John Oates (1975)
Personnel:
Daryl Hall: vocals, keyboards
John Oates: vocals, guitars
Chris Bond: guitar and synthesizer
Jim Gordon, Ed Green, Mike Baird: drums
Gary Coleman: percussion
Leland Sklar, Scotty Edwards: bass
Clarence McDonald: keyboards
Sara Allen: backing vocals
Recorded at Larrabee Sound and Western Sound Recorders, Los Angeles
Producers: Christopher Bond, Daryl Hall, John Oates
Release date: 18 August 1975
Label: RCA
Chart Placings: US: 17, UK: 56
Running Time: 35:20

Still not reaching the heights of being a headline act, Daryl and John opened for The Bee Gees in late February and early March 1974, before settling into the War Babies sessions mid-year, working on the album during June, and playing a concert with Todd Rundgren in New York's Central Park on 22 June to mark his 26th birthday. They did most of the heavy lifting promoting their final Atlantic album that October, on tour as support act for Lou Reed. It was an odd match at a difficult point in Reed's life, and 'a huge mistake and a terrible combination', according to Oates. 'Lou was at his lowest. He was stoned, and it was a match made in hell. We lasted four or five shows before we stopped'. Other sources suggest they stuck with the tour through to late November, including a trip across the border for a concert in Toronto on 19 October.

As Daryl and John were preparing to slog around the circuit as bottom of the bill, one of an increasing number of covers of their songs paid off, with R&B vocal group Tavares reaching the *Billboard* Hot 100,, and scoring a number one soul single, with their rendition of 'She's Gone', just as H&O were striking out in that very different direction.

War Babies proved to be a sidestep rather than a new direction, though that rock sensibility, tucked away but never too far from their minds, re-emerged later in the decade for their *Beauty On A Back Street* album, leaving them even more disparaged for it, the second time around. Oates has suggested the end was in sight when Atlantic signed fellow blue-eyed soulsters Average White Band, and perhaps the label saw in the AWB what they'd thought they'd invested in with Hall & Oates. Hall has the opposite view, telling *Shindig:* 'It was our decision to leave Atlantic for RCA'. John saw it as being about dollars – neither of them having yet taken an interest in the business side – and that the change came because 'It was our manager being greedy and wanting to make more money. RCA didn't really have a lot of artists, and there was an opportunity'.

What that meant, aside from a major label cash advance that must have made them feel like the big time was finally calling, was an opportunity to rethink the way forward, leading to their first singles-chart success. It saw them join forces again with *Abandoned Luncheonette* guitarist Christopher Bond, who this time played in the studio band and adopted the role of producer and arranger, with whom they'd have an increasingly tense relationship across their first three RCA albums. Engineering the sessions, Barry Rudolph, who'd worked with Bond on previous projects, recalled on his blog how 'Daryl and John wanted to do a new record, but they had no band (at least nobody they wanted on their record). Chris utilised a studio band and arranged and wrote out all the music for the players. Daryl and John also played on the tracking sessions, imparting their artistry to what could have turned out to be a sterile recording situation. [Vocally] they knew exactly what they wanted, where to do it, and most importantly, how to do it'.

Sessions came off the back of some early-1975 dates, where – as they had on the *War Babies* tour – they'd try out new material and attempt to find a fresh tone and style to inform their new recordings. Not a heavily-bootlegged live act, some of this trial and error work is lost to time, though a 4 February 1975 recording of a number called 'Hard To Compromise' – captured at the Roxy Theatre, Northampton, PA – glances across the pond to Britain's burgeoning pub rock scene, and has nothing in common with how they'd recrystallise their Philly-soul sound in the coming album sessions.

In *Rolling Stone*, Ben Edmonds wrote of *Daryl Hall & John Oates*: 'Finally ... a clear-cut style. Lean, basic, and more concerned with capturing the moment directly in sketchbook form than belabouring the point with involved brushwork. You'd be correct in saying that the first side is R&B and the second pop, but you'd be missing the point. Hall & Oates are a fusion of the two'. And in listening to the confident sheen that sits on the surface of these songs, it's clear that Christopher Bond *got* who they were and what they ought to be doing, just as Arif Mardin had done previously. After five years hard work, the chart success of the smouldering 'Sara Smile' – not to mention the recognition from the Tavares cover – allowed Atlantic to reissue 'She's Gone', and double that top ten success.

Then there was the album packaging to consider. The *Whole Oats* cover – an open can of 'Quick' Quaker Oats with the album title supplanting the brand name, against an orange background with Daryl Hall & John Oates headlined above – had made no suggestion of any band image, and many of their subsequent albums have featured straightforward visuals. *Abandoned Luncheonette* was an exception. The shot of the luncheonette left to rot and decay among the weeds alongside Route 724, and the internal black and white photography of Daryl and John seated in the diner, were shot by

Barbara Wilson, and are as poignant as the title track itself, with a melancholy aura that's still quite haunting fifty years later. The *War Babies* cover was by Californian designer/illustrator Peter Palombi, and was an eclectic mix of objects – from an Evenflo baby bottle to a political election badge for the 1952 Eisenhower/Nixon presidential ticket, Ritz crackers and family snapshots, all linking the album title back to the idea of being the last busted flush of the baby-boomer generation. But there'd been nothing in their catalogue so far that compared to the cover and internal photography for their first RCA album *Daryl Hall & John Oates*: forever known as the 'silver' album.

Created by former Elizabeth Arden staffer Pierre LaRoche – who helped develop David Bowie's Ziggy Stardust look and conceived the lightning-bolt face makeup for his Aladdin Sane persona, the 'silver' album cover is striking for its futuristic metallic sheen, for sure, but it's legendary and rather notorious for its gender-fluid glamorisation of John, and more particularly, Daryl. It added to the rumours and mystique surrounding their sexuality and made a powerfully edgy statement that stepped them outside of their previously rather loose and louche, slightly hippie, soul-pop vibe. John explained to Jaan Uhelszki in the August-1977 edition of *Creem*:

Up until our 'silver' album, we felt we hadn't given anyone any kind of image. We had made three diverse albums, and we hadn't used our faces or personalities on the cover, which wasn't great for trying to get any kind of image across. So, we decided to change all that, and went completely over the edge. At least we weren't being ignored anymore. It didn't hurt to try anything, was our philosophy. If you're not selling records, nothing is going to harm you.

He further elaborated in the 1984 biography *Dangerous Dances*: 'If we were going to put our faces on an album cover for the first time, we wanted to do it in a big way. Pierre said, in that French accent of his, 'I will immortalise you!'. And he did just that. To this day, it's the only album cover that people ask us about'.

'Camellia' (Oates)

On *Prosoundweb.com,* engineer Barry Rudolph recalls the duo's arrival at Larrabee Sound on the album's first recording day as being 'in sync and present'; Oates proclaiming 'We are cutting the album's first single today'. Rudolph says that without even cutting a demo, they knew 'Camellia' was going to be it, and reflects on how it was 'immediately obvious that both the artists and producer knew exactly what they wanted musically, and what it was supposed to sound like'.

Widely thought to have the album's clearest hit potential – a delicious blue-eyed soul confection with a light touch belying its bittersweet undertones – 'Camellia' sank without trace: a fate it shared with the next offering: the Oates solo-written 'Alone Too Long'. Producer Christopher Bond later voiced his scepticism, saying he'd 'cut 'Camellia' three different times with three different sections. I did two different string dates on it. I tried it with two different drummers. I even tried cutting it in different studios to see if I could make it sound like a hit to me, and it never did'.

Bond may not have thought the song was a hit, and the public proved him right, but it's hard to hear why. Catchy and infectious, possessing some super harmonies, and with a wistful and relatable story, it deserved to be a perennial in the H&O canon. Fortunately, there was such an evergreen song on the album.

'Sara Smile' (Hall, Oates)

John recalls how they actually had 'no intention of releasing 'Sara Smile' as a single. We thought it was a simplistic, beautiful little love song that didn't jump out as something that would be a big hit on the radio'. But the choice of Hall's timeless love letter to Sara Allen as the third single came as a delightful bit of serendipity at a point when they were putting the album in the past and starting to look towards the next record: 'We got a call from our manager saying that a small station in Ohio had chosen it as an album cut (to) tremendous response. And they communicated that to RCA ... and it became a big hit'. But not a chart-topper – in a slow burn from its 31 January 1976 release date, it reached number 4 in June. But it was enough for Atlantic to take another look at their H&O catalogue and reissue 'She's Gone', likely as the most similar track they held rights for. And off the back of that Tavares version, it reached number 7, riding on the coattails of 'Sara Smile'.

In the couple of years since Sandy Allen had made her first appearance in a Hall & Oates song – 'Las Vegas Turnaround' – she and Daryl had commenced a relationship that seems to have been somewhat on/off in nature, and despite never leading to marriage, lasted close to 30 years. Given their longevity and the influence Allen had on the duo's songwriting and photography, it's no wonder the pair are often thought of as soul mates. In Nick Tosches' 1984 biography *Dangerous Dances*, Sandy is portrayed as a mysterious, even peripheral figure, with the one photograph purporting to be her, showing only a figure in a beekeeper outfit to accentuate the secrecy. It's a little overplayed – a smattering of photos show her through the years with Daryl, and she was a 'talking head' contributor to a 1990s *Behind The Music* H&O documentary, even though Hall in 1984 described her as 'secretive alright!' and awkwardly talked of her as 'my roommate, live in... whatever you want to call it'.

Though it's a song that's co-credited to the duo, it's widely accepted that this one is largely Hall's, which Oates has confirmed: 'Over the years, I've always tacitly acknowledged that it was his song, because it was. But he and I wrote the lyrics together'. John, however, credits the music and chord changes, the melody and the chorus, written while financial necessity saw Daryl and Sara apartment-sharing with John in New York City, all to his musical partner.

Coming early in Daryl and Sara's years together, 'Sara Smile' is a gloriously simple love song that belies its surface's emotional uncertainties, but feeds on them in the lyrical doubts that keep creeping in. It's a song about infatuation, the first intense flush of passion and love, countered with insecurity and fear of loss. Curiously, Hall much later described it as a 'postcard to Sara Allen, who was my partner for many, many years, a 'having a great time, wish you were here' kind of thing.' In 2009, he told *American Songwriter*: 'When that song comes on, the reality hits that we're not together anymore, so it's a very poignant and hard thing for her to deal with. I can still sing that song today and feel real about it, and always will'.

'Alone Too Long' (Oates)
This song enjoyed a second lease of life as the theme to the 2013 Stephen Merchant sitcom *Hello Ladies*. Talking about it in hindsight, John made it sound as though the lyrics were semi-autobiographical rather than coming from his usual observational method: '[It] was a song about being a young, single and confused guy living in the big city, just trying to figure it all out ... who I was and if there was anyone out there for me'. If it's a song that feels somewhat slight, that's more to do with the high quality of the work that surrounds it than an inditement.

'Out Of Me, Out Of You' (Hall, Oates)
This is another of those mid-1970s songs that refer to the Philadelphia soul sound, which quintessentially lingers around Hall & Oates despite how they pushed the envelope with albums like *War Babies*. Vocals are geographically stretched to a complementary Californian vibe, and reverence is paid to Motown classics and Beach Boys harmonies. There's so much good stuff on this record, and, honestly, 'Out Of Me, Out Of You' is a lesser track, stretched and rather thin with a subdued production mix and a lyrical narrative that half-heartedly tails off well before the end.

'Nothing At All' (Hall, Sara Allen)
This is a curious song to be sharing an LP side with 'Sara Smile', since it's arguably even better. As Paul Pearson writes in his impressive advocacy of the H&O catalogue on *Treblezine.com*: 'With Hall's crooning about an anticlimactic ending, over Jim Gordon's quietly-spastic snare rattling', it shares something of the same imagery, with Hall declaring how 'We spent last night like every night/ Sitting and staring'. But while the nighttime setting of 'Sara Smile' starts a plea about staying 'until tomorrow', here it's part of a relationship simply winding down and running out of steam.

'Gino (The Manager)' (Hall, Oates)
In Ken Sharp's sleeve notes for the album's 2000 Buddha Records reissue, Oates says this song contains 'one of my favourite lyrics of all time. I think we captured something there, it's a moment in time'. Gino himself was, of course,

their long-term manager Tommy Mottola. 'He was just starting out in his career as we were just starting out in ours. We grew up together in the music business'. A glorious send-up or an affectionate tribute? It's very tongue-in-cheek as it portrays Mottola as the classic music biz manager with his 'Sign on the line/Sign on the line' insistence and his overarching self-importance – 'You couldn't live without little Gino, no' – though that view is quickly followed by the unconvinced, 'That's what he tells me, little Gino, no'.

It seems Mottola – who went on to become Sony Music CEO and husband of Mariah Carey – was happy to recognise himself in the song, once claiming, 'I thought it was true and I thought it was great', adding knowingly that 'You've probably heard stories about me. Some of them are true. Some of them aren't'.

Positioned as side-two opener, 'Gino (The Manager)' is part of the pantheon of songs about music business managers – Ramones' 'Danny Says' (though that's as much about Joey Ramone's girlfriend Linda Daniele as it is their manager Danny Fields), Queen's vicious 'Death On Two Legs (Dedicated To...)', and Julian Cope's 'Bill Drummond Said'. Mottola also appears in the 1976 disco-chart-topping 'Cherchez La Femme' by Dr Buzzard's Original Savannah Band, where he's portrayed as recently broken-up with his lady, living on the road, sleeping in the back of a grey Cadillac and 'Blowin' his mind on cheap grass and wine'. Ouch.

'(You Know) It Doesn't Matter Anymore' (Hall, Sara Allen)

After the cheeky aberration of 'Gino (The Manager)', here's another smooth and light Philly-laden tune, with Sara Allen putting in an appearance with some delicate backing vocals. These are mixed low in the harmonies but add a confidentiality to the song that gives it a sense of intimacy, suggesting that though it's Hall's lead vocal, the words have a very personal shared sentiment to them.

'Ennui On The Mountain' (Hall, Oates)

A strident, stompy soundtrack to a familiar yearning for the country life– we've heard their wish to get out of the city often by now - but without their earlier, more simple outlook, because success means that it needs to come with a thousand acres, so not just room for a pony but also for the roadies and girlfriends accoutrements. Ennui is a word that reflects a feeling of weariness and dissatisfaction, and its invoking here reflects again how disaffected with the music business they'd become, seeing it as just going round and round (like a record, baby!) for the dream of airplay and gold discs. Ponce de Leon – mentioned as an analogy representing that which can't ever be found – was a Spanish explorer who arrived in America on Columbus' second expedition and became governor of Puerto Rico. He charted the Atlantic coast to the Florida Keys, from which a likely apocryphal story grew that the voyage was undertaken in search of the mythical Fountain of Youth. Perhaps the duo had come to despair that their ambitions would be as elusive.

'Grounds For Separation' (Hall)

It's said that this song was an early choice for use in the movie *Rocky*. Sylvester Stallone said, 'I will admit, the first temporary tune I used for the *Rocky* montage was a tune written by Hall and Oates called 'Grounds For Separation'. This provided a direction for [score composer] Bill Conti to go'. With its boxing metaphor, 'I can fight with the best, but I can only go so many rounds', it's not hard to see why. A few years later, British glam rockers The Sweet had a similar lyric idea in their 'Love Is Like Oxygen' – 'You get too much, you get too high/Not enough and you're gonna die' – guitarist Andy Scott talking about love's emotional baggage. But Hall used the idea as a caution for the way music dominated his life: 'But isn't it a bit like oxygen/Too much will make you high'.

'Soldering' (Ewart Beckford, Alvin Ranglin)

A rare foray into reggae, Oates recalled this being the first time they'd experimented with a Roland drum machine. He discovered the song one night in Jamaica – in his memoir explaining his moment of epiphany when he cut through the 'hypnotic beat' being played on the beach, and caught up with the words' sexual metaphor. Driving to the nearest town the next day, he located a copy of the single – presumably the original by The Starlites – and took it to the studio. This cover version made both an interesting change of pace to end the second side on, and quite the juxtaposition for singles buyers flipping the sentimental and heartfelt 'Sara Smile' over to the sharp innuendo of 'Soldering' on its B-side. One wonders whether they thought that one through... or whether they saw it as a delicious joke?

Related tracks
'What's Important To Me' (Hall)

This was likely recorded in the initial early-1975 RCA sessions but abandoned when Daryl and John reconvened in June to work on the 'silver' album. The Buddha Records reissue added two demos, giving a tantalising glimpse of the duo starting out with their new label, away from the security blanket of arrangement guru Arif Mardin. Though coming across as incomplete, it does have a polished Daryl vocal featuring plenty of his stylised asides and repetitions, though it's rather meandering and if it had been dusted down for those June '75 sessions would have benefited from tweaking and sharpening up.

'Ice' (Oates)

Of the two liberated demos, 'Ice' is more of a work in progress; an Oates number you could just hear Mardin getting his hands on and bringing up to scratch for *Abandoned Luncheonette*. With its sad lament for lives fading away like ice in a cup, it thematically belongs with that album's title track. To a gentle jazz backdrop, John crams in a mass of lyric ideas – some almost spoken, and sometimes rushed to make them work within the meter. Unusually, he positions himself as the narrator and reflects the air of unhappiness he's professed to have endured in the 1970s: 'She said, you know Johnny/It's been such a long time since I saw that pretty smile of yours meet mine'.

Bigger Than Both Of Us (1976)

Personnel:
Daryl Hall: vocals, keyboards, synthesizer, mandola
John Oates: vocals, rhythm guitars, harmonica
Christopher Bond: lead guitar, keyboards, synthesizer
Tom Hensley: acoustic piano
Scotty Edwards, Leland Sklar: bass
Jim Gordon, Ed Greene: drums
Slugger Blue: 'G Kick' drums
Gary Coleman: percussion
Tom Scott: flute, saxophone, lyricon
Charles DeChant: saxophone
Recorded at Cherokee Studios, Hollywood, CA
Producer: Christopher Bond
Release date: 8 September 1976
Label: RCA
Chart Placings: US: 13, UK: 25
Running Time: 34:51

After an extensive US tour in October 1975, they ended the year with a run of shows at New York's Bottom Line (where they'd pretty much started the year, on some dates with Britain's impish Leo Sayer), and a further small tour running up to Christmas. But the following year would see an increase in their profile beyond the US.

Daryl Hall & John Oates became a top 20 US album, gaining them attention in Canada, and Europe, where it reached 13 in the Netherlands, and 56 as their first UK album-chart appearance. 'Sara Smile' and 'She's Gone' the following year also reached the UK top 50: modest successes that wouldn't be repeated until the 1980s. Following a trip to London for a headline gig at the New Victoria Theatre on 3 October 1975, and an 18 May 1976 appearance on the BBC's flagship serious-music show *The Old Grey Whistle Test*, was a busy May schedule, travelling first to West Germany to appear on the television show *Der Musikladen*, then to the UK for selected dates at Bristol's Colston Hall, Manchester's Free Trade Hall, Newcastle City Hall, Oxford, Birmingham, Brighton and another appearance at the New Victoria, ending in Leeds on 28 May.

Looking back at their lively, in-concert, OGWT performance, there's a clear distinction between the songs as recorded and a more college-rock delivery being developed on stage – such as for 'Camellia', where they allowed themselves an extended instrumental break as the coda for a sparkly, energetic take. A slick version of 'She's Gone' demonstrates how much Oates contributed to the sound and look, while Hall's vocal embellishments vividly showed off his range. There's some lovely mandolin work in the breakdown of 'Lady Rain', and a lead-guitar break from Todd Sharp in a band

43

assembled specifically for these dates. A delightfully wistful focus falls on Hall for 'Laughing Boy', and a spotlight on Oates for 'I'm Just A Kid' (also played on their German TV appearance), with some smart vocal duelling on a smoky jazz rendition of 'Is It A Star', leading to a no-nonsense blast through 'Gino (The Manager)' to round things off. *Melody Maker* said of a New York show at the end of 1976: 'They are terrific exponents of the lengthy, drawn-out climatic finish, producing great symphonies of sound that give their songs the elegant air of *major* works. The effect is always stunning'. It's an accurate assessment, showing how far their live shows were deviating from their studio sound.

But for UK audiences, they were still a well-kept secret - tickets for their Newcastle gig named them as 'Daryl Hall and John Oakes' - with *Melody Maker*'s Chris Welch, reviewing their second New Victoria show in London, saying how they were 'revisiting the scene of an earlier triumph' when 'the under-publicised, un-hyped vocal duo had achieved public acclaim', but considered them 'very much a preserve of the cognoscenti, with pockets of fans around the country'. What Welch enjoyed – apart from the band who were 'so good it hurt' – were the 'elements of sly humour, unashamed romanticism, a fleeting wave of the hand at bi-sexuality, and a curious mix of black and country music'. They were establishing themselves as an international act, with Welch declaring them a 'thoroughly original and supremely talented team who have just crept in through the back door'.

They'd already started on what would become *Bigger Than Both Of Us*, doing some exploratory but aborted work in February in New York, before relocating to California and Los Angeles' Cherokee Studios, to again hook up with Christopher Bond and his select band of studio musicians. John claimed: 'We got so much more out of Chris, and the musicians, by virtue of having done the 'silver' album. The communication was there from the beginning'. It's curious, though, that despite having a warmly-received live band, they were still seeing a need to distinguish between session musicians and those in the live band: 'We feel that by playing live and actually interacting with the real world, we can influence these guys in the studio ... help them relate to what's happening'. Conceding to British music journalist Chris Charlesworth that Bond had been a key component of *Abandoned Luncheonette*, despite Daryl's concerns with hearing Bond's Beatles fascination permeate the album's second side, John talked about what he saw as the positive evolution of their relationship: 'We figured Christopher would be the right person to bring it all together because he knew us and knew what we were trying to do. We just tried to consolidate what we thought were our strong points and establish a sound that people could recognise. Up until that point, we had a schizoid identity'.

In the same interview, Hall mooted that their next album might be a live one (It wasn't, though their first live album *Livetime* materialised in 1978), and started to talk about stretching his own creative legs: 'I'm thinking of doing a solo album, which is something I've been working towards for a long time. I want to be able to do Daryl Hall music: which is a bit different as far as I'm concerned. I won't say I'm more progressive, but it's something like that'.

'Back Together Again' (Oates)

Kicking the album off in a totally joyous way (though barely scraping the US Top 30 as follow-up to the hugely successful 'Rich Girl'), this isn't, as might be guessed at first glance, a self-congratulatory song title, but instead reflects John's delight at the resurgence of 1960s legend Frankie Valli, both as a solo artist and with The Four Seasons. It's a wide-grinning celebration of renewal and regeneration. Valli had rather fallen out of fashion in the socially and politically conscious 1970s, with new singles barely bothering the charts and an album rejected by Motown. Yet by 1975, he was, as Oates writes, 'back, riding high ... on everybody's dial', as first his chart-topping single 'My Eyes Adored You' and then The Four Seasons' 'Who Loves You' (number 3) saw Valli's profile rebound.

Aside from Oates' unrestrained delight at an artist from the old days finding his voice again, 'Back Together Again' is a validation that music isn't ephemeral; that it lives on and thrives beyond the generation that first finds it: 'Well the kids are all grown up/But their records are still alive'. Oates suggested to the website *Something Else Reviews* that the song reflected his and Daryl's doo-wop roots: 'I don't think a lot of people recognise that for what it is: urban folk music. Doo-wop is not too distinct from the old blues field-holler but set in an urban context. Rap music is the same ... music of the streets'.

'Rich Girl' (Hall)

Famously, this enduring H&O song, and their first number one, isn't about a girl at all, as Sara Allen recalled in that brief 1977 *Circus* magazine interview: 'Actually, 'Rich Girl' is a rich boy: someone I knew in Chicago. Daryl loves to write songs about my old boyfriends'. Naming the old boyfriend as Victor Walker, Jr., and describing him as a 'burnout', Hall said the germ of the song came from a visit Victor made to Daryl and Sara's apartment, where Walker was recalled as 'acting sort of strange ... This guy is out of his mind, but he doesn't have to worry about it because his father's gonna bail him out of any problems. But you can't write 'You're a rich boy', so I changed it to a girl'.

The song itself wasn't without its problems either. Even in the liberated 1970s, the use of the word 'bitch' ('It's a bitch girl/But you've gone too far') was an issue, as Hall recalled to the *LA Record*:

> There were a lot of stations that switched the word, turned it backwards, bleeped it. There was one station that – even when it was number one – wouldn't play it because it had the word in it. It sounds so quaint now. We were maybe the first bunch of people to ever have a number one record that had a bleeped word. We're ahead of our time!

That was nothing, however, compared to the bizarre, and, to be fair, totally unsubstantiated claims that the killing frenzy of mass murderer and self-titled

Son of Sam, David Berkowitz – he shot and killed six people between July '76 and July '77 – had been fermented by the melody to 'Rich Girl'. Hall has said he couldn't recall exactly how he came by this story: 'Maybe one of the detectives ... During the police interrogations with Berkowitz, he said he listened to 'Rich Girl' to motivate himself'. We'll hear more from Daryl on that in due course, but the perplexing part is that the first murder took place on 29 July 1976, whereas *Bigger Than Both Of Us* didn't get released until September, and the single wasn't released until the following January.

'Crazy Eyes' (Oates)
'It has to do with a young girl I was dating', said Oates, while playing an acoustic version at The Troubadour in 2018, organised by *Rock Cellar* magazine, 'and it was tumultuous, let's just say that'.

'Do What You Want, Be What You Are' (Hall, Oates)
For an interview with Ken Sharp in *Goldmine*, Daryl reflected on the title of this song, used for a career-spanning box set in 2009. 'That does encapsulate the way I think. John and I are both very individualistic. We share a view and that is a unique view, and it's hard for me to describe what it is, but it's not the same as most other people. I think we approach music that way. I'm not afraid to do things. Fear is one of those restrictive things that hold you back from fulfilment'.

'Kerry' (Hall, Stephen Dees)
A middle-of-the-road and very typical 1970s rocker, 'Kerry' has a bit of desperation about it, particularly in the 'Kerry, you can Kerry-on' lyrics that needed a pencil strike-through as soon as they got jotted down, they're that contrived. In a way, it's exactly what's wrong with this album – once you get past the joyous opener and the legendary hit, there's very little that's memorable, little that the 'silver' album didn't do a whole lot better. And so, four songs in, *Bigger Than Both Of Us* is treading water, despite Daryl at the time of its release claiming, 'Every song is a gem! It's gonna make our other albums look tame!'.

The song's co-writer Stephen Dees was a session musician working with the likes of Pat Travers and Todd Rundgren before cutting the solo album *Hip Shot* – produced by Daryl, who also played keyboards – then forming the early-1980s power-pop band Novo Combo with Santana drummer Michael Shrieve. *Hip Shot* includes Dees' own take on 'Kerry': similar to the H&O version, though if truth be told, at a more plodding pace.

'London Luck & Love' (Hall, Oates, Sara Allen)
An understated but happy tune about being in the right place and meeting someone with who you create an instant connection, this song is the quiet pleasure of side two: a charming ode to things that just feel *right*.

'Room To Breathe' (Hall, Sara Allen)

A messy heads-down barroom rocker, it's easy to imagine this one being built from a studio jam with the musicians all falling over each other to assert their own authority on proceedings and ending up as an unfocused rabble creating a jumbled muddle that must have been fun to record, but doesn't add anything here.

'You'll Never Learn' (Hall, Oates)

John's self-loathing delivery of this twisted and aggressive lyric ('Now don't you hate you in the morning/You'll never learn') do more to signpost the direction of the next album *Beauty On A Back Street* than they do to sit comfortably here, even alongside the barbed sentiments of the likes of 'Rich Girl'. At the coda, it boils up into a weird screech; a seeming judgemental view of someone's suicide attempt ('twisted medication', 'scars from the trial', 'razor queen'). It's a really difficult listen that has a companion piece in that following record's 'The Emptyness'.

'Falling' (Hall)

Outlasting any other track on the album by a good two minutes, 'Falling' is a highly adventurous genre-crossing piece with parts that could pass as the work of a 1970s Krautrock band (particularly the likes of Popol Vuh or Can), another Todd Rundgren-influenced moment, or a Brian Eno production. Sparse, tender and haunting, it builds to a crescendo of vivid lead guitars against sombre bass, Hall's voice echoing the title as it indeed falls out of the mix and the song breaks down into synthesizer experimentation. And if that suggests that this was an attempt to stretch recording boundaries – not to be replicated on stage – there's another 1977 German *MusikLaden* TV appearance where they stretch it out to an eight-minute progressive rock statement that's wholly indicative of the way in which they'd started, and would continue, to make their songs pliable for a live environment and not simply playing the record as heard on vinyl.

The album's envelope-pushing side two has a continuing sense that they don't really know what they want to be and are being pulled in different musical directions almost from one track to the next. Are they heading towards a mainstream rock sound? Do they want to embrace progressive rock (just at the absolute wrong moment when punk is about to sweep it aside), or do they want to expand on that folk and soul thing that's giving them chart recognition? They'd look back later and feel that the answer they found was absolutely the wrong one.

Beauty On A Back Street (1977)

Personnel:
Daryl Hall: vocals, keyboards, Polymoog synthesizer, guitar, mandolin
John Oates: vocals, rhythm guitars, mando-guitar, electric piano, dulcimer
Christopher Bond: backing vocals, keyboards, synthesizer, tonalities, six and twelve-string guitars
Scott Edwards, Leland Sklar, Jim Hughart: bass
Jeff Porcaro: drums, electronic drums
Gary Coleman: percussion, sound effects
Tom Scott: tenor saxophone
Tommy Mottola: backing vocals
Recorded at Cherokee Studios, Hollywood, CA
Producer: Christopher Bond
Release date: 11 October 1977
Label: RCA
Chart Placings: US: 30, UK: 40
Running Time: 36:34

If *Whole Oats* became their largely forgotten album, and *War Babies* their most stylistic, then *Beauty On A Back Street* is the one they came themselves to pretty much shun, with it being eschewed from compilations and even ignored on their massive career-retrospective set *Do What You Want, Be What You Are*. John told the *Burning Wood* blog: 'If you look very carefully, there's not one song from *Beauty On A Back Street* on this box set. I hated that album. We were recording with Chris Bond, and our relationship with him was deteriorating... that all came to its nadir at *Beauty On A Back Street*. It's probably the album I like... well, it's the album I hate'.

Hall recalled in a *Record Collector* interview that by this time, he was '[fighting] a lot with Bond, so I wasn't happy in the studio, but that's personal rather than objective. I only recall the bad stuff'. Oates, always more diplomatic and restrained, agreed in an interview conducted for their next LP: 'About halfway through the sessions, we realised our attitude was wrong. It was our last record with Christopher Bond, and not made in the best of personal circumstances'.

In 2001, Chris Bond – who'd by then left the music business – spoke to Mark Hershberger in an interview for a website devoted to Canadian progressive rock band Klaatu, who Bond produced in the early 1980s. He reflected on his production methods back in the day, talking about how, with Klaatu, it was important to him to find songs that worked together, and linking that back to his earlier production work.

There are at least two songs I can think of right now – Hall and Oates records – that have never been released, that are great songs, but they didn't fit the overall journey. One of them did get released later, on a compilation of those guys, Hall and Oates, because they were so confused... I mean, I did some really good things with them, and I did some things I didn't like so much. Some of my best work was there. We were a trio.

There's a hint of a suggestion in Bond's recollections that the disconnection between Daryl and John on the one hand, and their producer and long-time musical associate on the other, wasn't all one-way and perhaps indicated the stresses of success and the expectations that comes with it. They cut the album during what was a busy year, with a touring schedule far beyond what they'd previously experienced. They returned to London for another *Old Grey Whistle Test* on 11 January 1977, spending the rest of the month trekking around the UK, including two sold-out nights at the Hammersmith Odeon (one on 23 January being bootlegged on multiple labels), and a couple of dates in Scotland, before travelling to Bremen in West Germany for a second *Der Musikladen* appearance and a handful of European dates. That they then returned to London on 15 February for another Hammersmith show, tells us their time as a well-kept British secret was demonstrably over.

After recording the album in April, they toured it extensively across the US in June, July and October through to December, Hall working in August on his solo album *Sacred Songs* in New York with producer Robert Fripp.

In hindsight, it's clear to see that the whole year was a confusing experience. A major *Creem* piece by Jaan Uhelski that August, revealed the duo to be struggling with ego, fan attention and their sense of identity. Hall claimed, 'I want to be a rock star, that's all I care about', and bemoaned John for singing 'the same line over and over again for two hours', while John countered that, '(Daryl) sometimes has the delusion that he's asleep when he's awake ... he has trouble discerning whether he's asleep and dreaming he's doing something, or really doing it'.

In fact, 1977 was a transformative year that had to simply be endured, first yielding the end of their working relationship with Bond – severed off the back of an album they couldn't recognise themselves in, a Daryl Hall solo album that a horrified RCA refused to release (it eventually appeared in March 1980, Nick Tosche in *Dangerous Dances* noting that the label shelved it for not being commercial), and a tough autumn/winter touring schedule where audiences were on occasion quite sparse. Described as 'The most lavish production of their career', a contemporary interview said, 'There were concert nights when they were virtually singing to themselves'. Oates noted:

We sank a lot of money into it. The show was a monstrosity, a white elephant. It was our stab at the big production syndrome. We had a huge computer-operated star that flashed in a thousand combinations on the nights that it was working. The fact that the record wasn't doing well hurt us badly.

They'd embarked on the tour with high hopes. 'I want to get closer to the essence of whatever is in the song when they're created,' said Hall at the time.

'The initial energy and tension. I like a lot of feeling in music, and the original feeling always gets diluted in the studio. We've lived in New York for six years now, so I feel the musical essence of the city ... the *vibe* of the city'.

In an October interview, at the start of the tour, John complained, 'We're never home. We live in New York, but we record in L.A., and the rest of the time, we're on the road. The few weeks I spent in New York, I was very happy. I was constantly busy; I was seeing my friends. All of a sudden, I'm transplanted out here'. To fill the gaps and remove himself from the music business, he'd expanded his long-held passion for motor racing – Formula One in particular – doing some amateur racing himself, while Daryl had been investigating the occult world of Aleister Crowley: 'People have to think about this stuff. They have to open their minds. It's not really to be discussed, but I'm going through your basic magical training initiation'. They'd made a record as dark as Hall's current fascination suggested. But a return to brighter material, and a new direction that would lead them to regular chart success, was just around the corner.

'Don't Change' (Hall, Oates)
Described by Daryl as 'like Bad Company, straight-ahead, hip-shot rock', the greatest sin that 'Don't Change' has as an album opener is that it's pretty flat... consider 'Back Together Again' on their previous outing, and fast forward to 'It's A Laugh' on the next to come, and here's a song that sets a tone that's uninspired, and a lyric with a self-satisfied twist where the protagonist, meeting this crazy new love interest at what's claimed to be the right moment, seems to want to ensure his scarlet women doesn't change until the pay-off coda 'don't change *my* life'.

'Why Do Lovers Break Each Other's Heart?' (Hall, Sara Allen)
Described by one blogger as 'a generic 1950s-inspired Four Seasons kinda thing', this is arguably the odd one out on the album. Sounding like it has continuity with the 'silver' album and *Bigger Than Both Of Us*, and less off-kilter than its surrounding numbers, even though it feels underdeveloped and lightweight. Given Daryl and Sara's complex commitment to each other, it comes across as two sides of a story: each reaching for words that might explain something to the other. With Hall singing both parts, the female character bitterly recalls the other women present in the couple's time together and the lack of commitment and understanding. The impatient male clearly fails the empathy test: 'Crying and laughing/Does she love the pain?'. There's an honest song idea being explored here, but it feels more like an abandoned work-in-progress than something that should've been released at all, let alone culled as the LP's first single, reaching as it did an underwhelming 73 in the States.

'You Must Be Good For Something' (Hall, Oates)
A strident rocker filled with loathing and bile, this is one of those introspective songs that could be about the duo's relationship with the music business: a

theme Daryl particularly returned to in several instances. Oates claimed in one interview: 'We were talking to ourselves in that song'. Hall told *Circus* it was 'based on a late-60s type modal riff. It's manic. It actually gets *hysterical*'.

Situation hollow
Loving chained to dollars
I can't live with your totalitarian standards

Everything about this song is a churned-up gut-wrench: porn on cable television; swapping K-mart clothes for Dior off the back of churning out that number one hit night after night as though the lyric sheet is on autocue, and embracing the lowest common denominator. The protagonist lashes out, claiming to be out of time, or in other words, out of step with the industry as it has become, asserting that he'll never be like the subject of the song. Oates noted: 'When you look at the sentiment behind (the title), it was a low point, honestly. Through the prism of my own experience, if you're low and down, depressed and not satisfied with not only your life but where you're at, the whole experience is going to be coloured by that'.

'The Emptyness' (Oates)
The sparse and mournful piano that opens this, the build-up into a power ballad, and then into a moment of reflective introversion, almost nursery rhyme in texture, has something of Queen and Freddie Mercury in its construction. Oates had been taking piano lessons prior to the sessions, describing playing keys as giving him a whole new sense of harmonics: 'It's easier to manipulate and articulate chord inversions. My first piano ballad, 'The Emptyness''.

Though it's ostensibly a lament for love lost and heartache that only reunion can ease – or as John put it: 'Wanting to come home to someone' – it reflects both the album's mood and a state of despair that John acknowledges was hanging over him like a black cloud:

I can't honestly say I was very happy in the '70s. I was a different person, and I'm completely different now. I've grown and matured so much, but in those days, honestly, happiness wasn't a big part of my life. Success was, and career and creativity were running my life, and being happy wasn't a big part of it. Daryl and I were never really satisfied, and happiness really took a back seat to what was going on in our lives. We had this big machine that was being created around us. We're both much happier individuals now.

'Love Hurts (Love Heals)' (Oates)
This is another track that comes across more like a sketch of an idea than a fully-formed song. John's rumination on a relationship heading for the rocks, loses its way by the middle, and plays out as a repetitive refrain lifted from

the initial chorus. By this point, *Beauty On A Back Street* is starting to feel laboured, and Oates recollection of it not being made in the best of personal circumstances, starts to resonate.

'Bigger Than Both Of Us' (Hall, Oates)

Respite from what's turned into a rather stodgy dirge comes with what sounds like it's a leftover from the album of the same name, and has often been quoted as such, though, asked on an Internet chat, the answer is recalled more simply, Daryl liked the album title and resurrected it after the fact for a song.

'Bad Habits and Infections' (Hall)

This has more aggressive and angular chords, more combative and angry lyrics, and a strange middle section that briefly sounds like Sparks. Daryl explained this rocker as comparing a former girlfriend to a terminal disease: 'She will know who she is', he haughtily declared. Dissolving into eldritch screeching in its 'I am the doctor' coda, it's a nasty song with unhealthy dependency at its core, and feels as ugly as Hall's summation suggests.

The song closed the set on the album tour, and *The Lantern* reviewer Dorothy Gast – watching the band at St John Arena, Columbus, Ohio on 13 October 1977 – described the theatrical excess: 'Daryl came onstage wearing a doctor's white jacket ... Oates reappears also clad like a doctor, and carrying a huge syringe. Oates attacks Hall with the syringe, and Hall begins stumbling and falling but puts up a fight as Oates tries to pull him up a stairway to the rear of the stage. Oates finally wins out over the weakened Hall, putting him onto a high platform in front of an eight-pointed star. The star opens, the two performers fall into it, and the lights go out as the song ends the performance'. Clearly, the days of Daryl and John's cool Philly-soul had never been as far away as at that moment.

'Winged Bull' (Hall)

'Winged Bull' reflects Daryl's interest in the occult, and is a grand psychedelic/ progressive folly, invoking the Egyptian gods Ra and Isis, the trickster Pan, and what might be the ancient Assyrian deity Lamassu: with the head of man, eagle wings and the frame of a bull. 'A mystical Celtic thing', said Hall, 'Very religious and magical.' Sonorous and cathedral-like, the lyrics might be better described as mystical claptrap, another sign of the indulgence that had permeated this record. He'd later dismiss his interest in the works of Aleister Crowley, which seemed to inform this song, as being something 'a lot of people go through. I went through it and I retained a lot of it, and I discarded a lot of it. My life was unbalanced at the time'.

'The Girl Who Used To Be' (Oates)

John described this as his Hollywood number: 'Everyone has to write one ... all L.A. atmosphere, like trying to cross Ventura Boulevard at 4:00 a.m. while cars sail by with their power windows sealed tight'. It's no surprise that the end of this gritty LP isn't all glamour and flashbulbs, but the story of another failed silver-screen career, a child star whose moment stalled, consigning her to fleeting glimpses of re-runs and a life of wanting those second chances that never arrive. Quiet, reflective and sympathetic in a way that other songs on this record certainly are not, 'The Girl Who Used To Be' tugs at the heartstrings with a genuine sense of pathos. Having studied hard, expanding his musical knowledge into classical and adopting the piano, this is a great snapshot of John Oates maturing as a songwriter.

Along The Red Ledge (1978)

Personnel:
Daryl Hall: vocals, keyboards,
John Oates: vocals, guitars
Kenny Passarelli: bass
Caleb Quaye: lead guitar
Roger Pope: drums
David Kent: synthesizer
Charles DeChant: saxophone
Additional musicians: George Bitzer, Rick Nielsen, Steve Lukather, Steve Porcaro, Robert Fripp, Todd Rundgren, Steve Foreman, Les Thompson, Jay Graydon, Dick Wagner, George Harrison
Arrangements: Daryl Hall, John Oates, David Foster
String arrangement on 'I Don't Wanna Lose You': Gene Page
Recorded at Davlen Sound, LA; Sunset Sound, LA; Hit Factory, New York
Producer: David Foster
Release date: 21 August 1978
Label: RCA
Chart Placings: US: 27, UK: -
Running Time: 36:49

If the earlier singles-chart success stalled through the unapproachable density of *Beauty On A Back Street*, then *Along the Red Ledge* only modestly placed the duo back in the chart's upper reaches, with its opener, 'It's A Laugh', managing a *Billboard* appearance at 20, though the follow-up 'I Don't Wanna Lose You' did not trouble the top 40.

The strength of *Along The Red Ledge* is as an album anyway. It feels like a pivotal moment – a closing of the first half of their RCA contract, with a return to the light touch that seemed to desert them, but with a newfound maturity and a sense of melancholy that permeates through the record from the get-go through to its haunting and atmospheric closing song.

They both found the results a particular highpoint, John suggesting on the *Burning Wood* blog that it marked them starting 'to rebuild and to lead to producing ourselves, which is where we had our most commercial success', and reflecting on how the journey 'kind of went up and went down and went up again'. It signified a change in the way they worked, with David Foster replacing Chris Bond, performing a task – perhaps unintentional at the outset – of being the conduit by which they'd start to find their way to producing themselves rather than being assistant producers to someone else's overarching vision. But it's also the moment they finally realised that the notion of their touring band being separate from the studio work was holding them back from a cohesive sound. But it was a tentative change, with many players who'd come to be synonymous with Hall & Oates, yet to arrive. A quick glance at the credits for *Livetime* – released in May 1978 and culled from a show in Hershey, Pennsylvania in 1977 – reveals a trio of former Elton-John-band musicians (Caleb Quayle, Kenny Passarelli and Roger Pope) and soon to be ever-present saxophonist Charles 'Mr Casual' DeChant transferring across to the studio for *Along The Red Ledge*. Oates acknowledged: 'This group is the best. Consequently, Daryl and I have been able to concentrate more on our singing and performing, and the music comes off livelier'.

That didn't mean that there weren't a plethora of additional musicians. They were at the point where they could call on friends and others for specific tracks – some of the players included George Harrison, Robert Fripp, and Cheap Trick's Rick Nielsen, who flew to L.A. after his band's April 1978 Japanese tour. He recalled to *Trouser Press*: 'They called and asked if I could come out and play. They were quoted in an article after our first album came out, saying that they thought highly of us. I'd never spoken to them, but they wanted some 'garbage-can sound' guitar, so I went out there and played for about eight hours. I played on four songs'.

They'd initially approached David Paich of the newly-formed Toto to handle production, with Tommy Motolla eventually contracting David Foster – a Canadian who'd go on to be Oscar-nominated and win multiple Grammy awards – who considered his Hall & Oates appointment to be 'a bit of a misfit. Daryl was into his rock period, and I was into my R&B period. I'd just come off working with Earth, Wind & Fire. We clashed a lot. I don't think he thought I was the right person for the job, even though we wound up doing two records together'. Foster, who previously played with Canadian band Skylark on their 1973 hit single 'Wildflower', went on to become a notable figure, responsible for records by The Tubes, Whitney Houston, Michael Bublé, Andrea Bocelli and Celine Dion. But *Along The Red Ledge* came at the start of his move into production. John recalled in our 2011 interview:

People don't realise, David Foster is such a famous producer, but the first album he ever produced was *Along The Red Ledge*, and after that, we worked together on *X-Static*. But during those recordings, he said to us, 'Why am I here? You guys are making this record'. And we said, 'Yeah, we kind of are, and that's what we're going to be doing in the future'. Which led directly to *Voices*.

A contemporary interview talked about their perceived four-steps-forward/three-steps-back career to date, with Oates asserting, 'Because we're songwriters as well as performers, we've got more staying power than most pop artists. We don't feel that pressure situation, the need to take the money and run'. So while *Along The Red Ledge* was to become quite a pivotal album that the duo saw as a particular highlight, it's also a stepping stone: a 'potpourri on the ledge' as Mark D. Director of *The Harvard Crimson* described it. Mind you, that review characterised the album as showing why 'Hall and Oates mania will never sweep the country ... they have some characteristic sounds, they can play formula pop, but not everyone likes their use of different styles of music. And *Along The Red Ledge*, in the end, becomes a Hall and Oates sampler, offering a little something for everyone'.

'It's A Laugh' (Hall)

A breath of fresh air blows through the album opener and lead single. That's partly from Charlie DeChant's triumphant return after being missing in action since *Bigger Than Both Of Us,* and from Hall rediscovering his mojo on a song that he declared himself to be 'very proud of. That song is very real. It's about a direct experience, and it has some surprises in it in terms of the chord changes'. John saw it as the Hall song he wished he'd written, describing it to *Goldmine* as 'one of my favourite Daryl songs. That song has a tinge of anger to it, which I really like. The song is in two different keys. The verse is in a different key than the chorus ... very unusual'.

It's arguably the best H&O breakup song – a plaintive cry lamenting the distance that's developed in a long-term relationship: 'You remember me/I used to be your boyfriend'. Alternating between the protagonist reflecting he 'really thought that we were special' and how 'Everyone thought we were forever', it's a brooding slice of regretful desperation, that perfectly sets the album's tone of loss, be that loss reflected as melancholy or loss wrapped up in nostalgia. Released as the LP's first single (b/w 'Serious Music'), it improved on the patch of poorly performing singles since 'Rich Girl' but still only landed at number 20 in the US. Perhaps it's that key change into the chorus, where Daryl appears to have one more word (around 'and the funny thing is…') than the melody could take, that made it feel out of step for a radio audience, but it's a stone-cold classic despite its low profile back in the day. There's an absolutely blinding live version – filmed in 1979 at the Stanley Theatre, Pittsburgh – that's well worth seeking out on YouTube.

'Melody For A Memory' (Oates)

Less exuberant, more orchestrated and yet more understated, this is another breakup number. It goes for the heart with a fatalistic sense of a relationship that one person has transcended and moved on from – the other lamenting the loss but always wanting to carry something of it in their heart; an easygoing, comfortable place where once there was 'Love in the morning/Love in the late afternoon'. Though it starts with the man's viewpoint, there's a temporary switch mid-song to a third-party observational voice that suggests the end *hasn't* been instigated by the woman:

> She cried when he left her
> Her eyes went black with the blue
> The infrequent letters
> The sooner the better

It's a mature and thoughtful song that seems to say love must let go sometimes to let someone blossom. Oates may not have been continually prolific, but when he had something to say, his realisations were often their albums' quiet highlights.

'The Last Time' (Hall)
Three tracks in, and it's still all about breaking up, relationships teetering on the edge and disbelief of something coming to an end – this time with a classy and lush Phil Spector production tone, and the appearance of George Harrison. Harrison had worked with David Foster when he played keyboards on George's *Thirty Three & 1/3* album. But that's coincidental, as the contact came from John Oates, who'd met Harrison in a roundabout way completely unconnected to music: an embryonic second career in motor racing, with the pair introduced to each other by three-times Formula One champion Jackie Stewart. Oates recalled:

> George and I bonded, not so much over music, but over Formula One racing. He was living in L.A. in the '70s ... I told him we were making an album, and asked him if he would play on it, and he was so cool – 'Only if I can just be in the band', and that's what he wanted to do: not to be singled out or have any special treatment.

'I Don't Wanna Lose You' (Hall, Oates)
A sharp string arrangement opens the song that was culled as the album's second single. This came with a lot of expectation of finding the next 'Rich Girl', only to have a modest chart impact. As Hall recalled to *Something Else Reviews*: "'I Don't Wanna Lose You' is a good one. It's like, here it is, this Philly song: it had all the elements. I said, 'This has gotta be a radio song', and it didn't get any response whatsoever'.

'Have I Been Away Too Long' (Hall)
This is built around Daryl's agile vocal, almost to the point of being a showcase for his voice, with harmony backing and the occasional angular lead guitar screech in the background. It closes side one with a hint that the second side will deliver more experimental work, another instance of the duo digging around for commercial tunes on side one and stretching themselves thereafter. But it's a counterpoint to the sequence of breakup songs, caught in the dilemma of whether to rekindle a past relationship and wondering out loud if the passage of time has left anything recognisable. Glorious anticipation – 'You're so close, I almost feel you breathing' – meets the potential of 'playing with disaster', and the tumult that this dichotomy brings is found in every note that Hall lets rip.

'Alley Katz' (Hall, Oates)
A strange jumble of frantic scattergun vocals, and what *Billboard* described as a 'sound close to punk' (They thought the same of the next track 'Don't Blame It

57

On Love', and how that got arrived at is anybody's guess), this track has what's also described as an 'emphasis firmly on rock 'n' roll, with driving guitars and pounding drums vying for attention in the mix with the pair's dynamic vocals'. Perhaps it's a backward glance to celebrate running with the gang; a paean to street friendships, though a contemporary critique thought it a mocking of 'the violent, socially rebellious lyrics of punk'. Either way, the manic glam-rock riffs and helter-skelter words bring the album a total change of pace. A unique song in the Hall & Oates catalogue.

'Don't Blame It On Love' (Hall, Oates)

While Oates is credited as having chipped in on the lyrics, this is clearly a Daryl song, influenced by his work the previous year with King Crimson's Robert Fripp, who appears on this track. They met a few years earlier, introduced through a mutual contact , and became friends immediately. Daryl recalled: 'I was starting to spend a lot of time in England, so I would stay at his house and he used to stay at mine. We have a lot of the same interests and we just got along'.

With an innovative but distinctly uncommercial Fripp-produced Daryl Hall album in the can, and a growing friendship between the two – not to mention the perceived mire of *Beauty On A Back Street* – a certain blonde head was being turned away from his long-time moustached compatriot and towards someone with substantial progressive-rock credibility. It seems like both sides became disillusioned even before Hall's *Sacred Songs* appeared in the racks, as Fripp told *Best* magazine that Hall and Oates 'limit their format and possibilities on purpose as part of a commercial compromise they accept', while in a 2007 *Pitchfork* interview, Daryl backtracked on his previous enthusiasm, claiming 'Robert, I think, had visions that he was going steal me away from John. That was never my intention'.

But that still leaves the tape-loop 'Frippertronics' of 'Don't Blame It On Love', and *Sacred Songs,* as milestones in their short-lived collaboration. It's a proper rocker with a muscular riff, and a lingering question – 'Who d'ya think your heroes are?' – that the *Voices* track 'Big Kids' would have a crack at answering a couple of years later.

'Serious Music' (Oates, George Bizter)

Two years on from the *joie de vivre* of 'Back Together Again' (John's celebration of popular music's permanence), he's surveying from a very different angle: seeming to despair at the chin-stroking musos sat in rapt attention for what he's describing as 'manuscripted memories' and 'sound with no electricity'. Where has he cast his gaze for this? Are the 'rows of robot symphonies' a reflection of electronic soundscapes from the likes of Kraftwerk? In his memoir, he referenced the stern-faced determination that inhabits serious music, from the classical orchestras to his beloved bluegrass musicians. But then there's the claim that 'Your rhapsody in blue will outlive us all', leading many to hear in the song a cleverly woven George Gershwin tribute, complete with a hazy and glamourous dream sequence leading into the middle eight. It's a glorious song, made more intriguing through its ambiguity.

'Pleasure Beach' (Oates)

Invoking nostalgia and melancholy in equal measure, carefree days of yore captured in rose-tinted hindsight, 'Pleasure Beach' – with its opening lament, Wurlitzer keyboards, screaming saxophone and hedonistic 'You for you and me for me' fantasies ultimately acknowledging it as something that exists in dreams, out of reach and unattainable – is perfectly positioned to set up the listless album closer 'August Day'. It's all described with John's keen journalistic eye:

> 'Pleasure Beach' was inspired by a girlfriend who had done a photo essay on an abandoned amusement park, and I thought that was really intriguing; a metaphor for a time gone by, a more innocent time, but also a slightly macabre kind of thing: a place where people had celebrated life, but were now gone from.

'August Day' (Hall, Sara Allen)

Although Daryl has described Sara Allen's songwriting as 'jumping into my thoughts and helping me to sort of coalesce them', there are a few songs where the demarcation between music and lyric are clearly defined. 'August Day' is a particular instance of that: Hall crediting the lyrics in full to Allen. And what evocative lyrics and atmospheric music this possesses – the perfect final song for an album that's so wrapped up in feelings of loss and things long gone.

Opening with an electronic sparseness that's more like the Brian Eno of *Another Green World*, it hangs as heavy as close weather – thunder out on the horizon, languid heat loitering in its keyboards – described through Allen's precise lyrics. Have there ever been better lines on any of Daryl and John's records than the distilled listlessness contained in 'Stir the dust and carve a rhyme' or 'Distant thunder and the slow dance/Static lightning daring me to take a chance'? It's a little piece of genius, minimal yet full of mood, involving and quite perfect.

RCA Years Part Two

X-Static (1979)

Personnel:
Daryl Hall: vocals, keyboards, synthesizer, vibraphone, mando-guitar
John Oates: vocals, guitar
G. E. Smith: guitar
John Siegler: bass
Jerry Marotta: drums
Charles DeChant: saxophone
Recorded at The Hit Factory, New York
Producers: David Foster, Daryl Hall
Release date: 1 November 1979
Label: RCA
Chart Placings: US: 33, UK: -
Running Time: 40:41

Though they traditionally recorded away from their New York homes, *Along The Red Ledge* had included some work at New York's Hit Factory, and it was becoming ever more important to the duo that they anchor themselves where they felt most comfortable; contemporary interviews constantly revealing their unhappiness with having to travel to California for sessions. Their next record, still with David Foster at the helm, saw them fully relocate to the Hit Factory and realign their sound to embrace the pop end of the new wave that was the softer legacy of punk. That's not to say they adopted new wave wholesale, more that it sits in the album's grooves as more of a background acceptance of the changing times, while what became *X-Static* was also informed by disco – punk's ubiquitous antithesis – and the emergence of disco's younger and wilder street-level sibling, hip-hop.

Being in New York, they were exposed to the music revolution that centred around Hilly Kristal's legendary East Village club CBGB – beloved of Ramones, Blondie, Talking Heads and Television – even though H&O's long-time publicist Jonathan Wolfson recalled how, taking on the role in the 2000s, he found 'the same cliched rock critics saying, 'Well, you didn't play CBGBs in 1978'. It was kind of bullshit, really'. Of course, those critics were technically correct that they weren't a part of that, though John has declared the impact of seeing Tom Verlaine and Richard Lloyd's Television at CBGB, and described to Chris Epting (co-writer of John's memoir) how, despite 'lots of bands starting to make noise in the city ... for me, it was all about Television'. He'd poke about in the depths of New York's underground scene, doing some production work for a long-forgotten band called Billy's (or possibly The Billies), and sitting in with punk and art-rock experimentalist Judy Nylon, who in 1974 had been the subject of the Brian Eno song 'Back In Judy's Jungle'. At least *some* of this can be heard buried deeply in the pop sheen of *X-Static*.

As Daryl asserted in a 1980 radio interview:

It's an approach we feel very comfortable with; that stark, lean and bare central approach, which we've always liked. New York and London music is really what it is. I don't call it new wave because that's too broad a statement, but it's New York and London music, and we're in New York, so we're part of it from that end. It's people being brave enough, in some cases, or non-talented enough in other cases, not to care about how much money they would make and just do whatever they wanted to do.

Billboard considered the result 'a solid effort, crisply produced by David Foster, and tightly played by some crack musicians', and although there was a slew of session players, the idea of a Hall & Oates band had really coalesced by this point, with G. E. Smith, John Siegler, Jerry Marotta and Charles DeChant giving the duo a bedrock they'd never had with their previous revolving cast of studio and live players. The *Billboard* review clearly felt they were getting somewhere with 'a harder-edged rock-disco sound that is at times brilliant', but also contended that it was 'dragging its feet a little bit at other times, especially when the twosome does straight disco'.

A later CD reissue promo sums up the album succinctly:

On 1979's *X-Static*, Daryl Hall & John Oates achieved perhaps the perfect marriage of blue-eyed-soul roots, infused with a wide-eyed, futuristic, avant-garde sensibility. Against the landscape of the impending new wave movement, *X-Static* exuberantly draws elements from Daryl's adventurous solo foray *Sacred Songs*, punk rock, and the percolating funkified street sounds of the urban jungle. The album resonates with an accessible, commercial sheen, laying the groundwork for Daryl and John's remarkable success in the '80s.

Yes, it's marketing hype, though retrospectively, it's pretty on the nail for a record that's another often overlooked part of their catalogue. But, at the time, they were still building back their following after the disappointing audiences noted on dates promoting the *Beauty On A Back Street* album, sometimes playing double early/late shows at smaller venues like San Francisco's Old Waldorf and The Roxy in Los Angeles.

X-Static was only a minor success in the album charts, and its singles ('Wait For Me' aside, which grazed the US top 20,) fell flat. The duo started to get the feeling that the next album would be their make or break moment.

'The Woman Comes And Goes' (Hall)

X-Static is a selection box of genres and styles, built upon the pop end of disco, with a definite glance at what was happening in the UK with the transition from punk rock to its more-palatable new wave sibling. But you wouldn't guess that from the stodgy opening track with its theme of casual friends-with-benefits sex, with the unnamed woman described as turning up in the narrator's life purely for her own kicks and leaving again 'when she's satisfied'. It's clunky and plodding, and, honestly, a bit misogynistic in hindsight, and certainly not a scene-setter for the rest of the album.

'Wait For Me' (Hall)

This bursts out like something from a Hollywood musical. It's always tempting to hear any Hall song in the context of his relationship with Sara Allen, its longevity belying a sense that the strains and temptations of a musician's life on the road always took a toll on the two of them. It's an articulation of guilt and a plea for understanding and patience in a romance described as having its light 'fading fast'. Daryl described it as 'one of the best songs I ever wrote', and it's such a heartfelt lyric, David Foster's big production sonically illustrating it so magnificently that it's hard to believe it doesn't come from somewhere deep inside and is representative of a moment in time. In the liner notes for the box set *Do What You Want, Be What You Are*, Hall conceded at least that 'I was feeling a certain way. I sat down and wrote the song and there it is'.

Alternatively, of course, the 'magic pair' that the song claims time is running out for could be Daryl and John themselves, having been mired in a run of releases that had failed to live up to expectations. They'd both talked of how difficult some of the 1970s had been, so a perfectly reasonable take on 'Wait For Me' might be as an analogy for *their* situation, particularly with Daryl having been working on his Robert Fripp side-project, a deliberation of whether to continue onwards that would culminate in what they later viewed as the make-or-break *Voices*.

'Wait For Me' should've been a smash hit, but – taken as the album's third single – its highest US chart position of 18 was something of a letdown. David Foster reflected how 'I helped provide the bridge that propelled them to their great commercial success ... disappointed for not being the one that actually produced the *big* songs for them'. His work with Daryl and John deserved greater recognition than either *Along The Red Ledge* or *X-Static* afforded him.

'Portable Radio' (Hall, Oates)

Yes, there really was a time in the 1970s when the portable radio was worthy of eulogising in song, and here Daryl and John take turns in extolling its virtues, and nice it is to hear their contrasting singing voices. Hey, portable radios are so great – you can check the sports scores, take one to the beach; it'll play music for the congregation or some no-nonsense rock 'n' roll for the youth. The mobile/cell-phone generation won't believe how liberating this device was! Just great fun, and an example of how *X-Static* embraced the pop generation in a way that Hall & Oates hadn't really done previously.

'All You Want Is Heaven' (Oates)

A big, bold production number for a saccharine-sweet delivery that manages to say nothing very much. Is it a lament for not being able to give enough to a partner? It's unclear and contradictory, and in truth, its starting point was as one of John's introspective mood pieces. But in the realisation, the glamourous arrangement missed the mark, and the musical-theatre harmonies are completely at odds with the words.

'Who Said The World Was Fair' (Hall, Sara Allen)

This venture into disco is a clear marker of *X-Static*'s scattergun approach to defining the duo's new direction, and like much of the album, the catchy melodies and upbeat rhythms work: all bright, shiny and infectious. You can imagine dancing to it, even while Hall gets across his anti-materialist message of the unseen but ubiquitous 'they' who would charge you for the sun shining up in the sky if they could find a way. It even manages to work-in imagery of the 1970s oil crisis: long queues for gasoline. Daryl's getting a bit political, eh? A funky lead-in sets the feelgood beat and from there on, it's all arms-in-the-air light touch fun, even with the preachy message in the lyrics.

'Running From Paradise' (Hall, Sara Allen)

Sitting astride the funky slap bass of this six-minute epic is a rather kinky tale of mirrored ceilings and sexual fantasy: an idea that never gets properly developed. There's probably a nicely risqué little song struggling to free itself from the bonds and handcuffs of this overproduced and unfocused ramble. It's six minutes of absolute filler that never goes anywhere.

'Number One' (Hall)

In a retrospective piece for *The Guardian*, Paul Lester had the intriguing and possibly validating notion that *X-Static* and its immediate successor *Voices* were akin to an American take on the highly-regarded British art-rock band XTC. Oates said, 'New wave and disco were happening. We recreated it through our own prism. I loved the angularity of that stuff'. *X-Static* definitely has a new wave influence, but the angularity Oates mentions is most evident on 'Number One', which, rather than being XTC-influenced, is more like the reggae/jazz stylings of The Police – that sparse sound where every vocal and instrument sounds separate from everything else – a gossamer anti-wall-of-sound that has a totally different energy to the surrounding tracks.

'Bebop/Drop' (Oates)

After all the poppy goodness and the Sting-lite diversion, Oates is adding some muscular rock on 'Bebop/Drop' with its urgent bass line, furious drums, and gritty, making his presence felt, guitar from new boy G. E. Smith. In the song, Oates's girlfriend - a casual or new attachment - is a 3 am night-owl wanting to live the party life; John just wants to get some sleep. The juxtaposition results in this febrile and frantic near hard-rock, quite punkish, bit of glam thrown-in salvo, with Oates memorably blasting out the vocals in a way that's quite different to his usual style.

'Hallofon' (Hall)

Most unusually is this brief instrumental interlude: one that Art of Noise might have been proud of. It's a noir-ish theme with an insistent backbeat that feels like it just needed an extra melody to merge into, and it could have been a 1970s cop show signature tune.

'Intravino' (Hall, Oates, Sara Allen)

As raucous and quirky as 'Pleasure Beach', 'Intravino' is a brilliantly fun way to see the album out, from the frantic intro's duelling guitars and keyboards, to Daryl s lauding of Beaujolais and Pouilly-Fuissé – though when he declares his adoration of their 'ruby colour', he overlooks that the latter is a dry white. While the song disdains whiskey – either of the scotch or rye persuasion – Hall has professed to mix a mean Old Fashioned as a bourbon drinker, saying that his home bar is 'mostly brown liquor: Ryes, bourbons, scotches, calvados. All the normal stuff, just good versions'.

Related Tracks

'Time's Up (Alone Tonight)' (Hall, David Foster)

A demo that emerged on some of the *X-Static* CD reissues, and a perplexing omission from the album. It could've worked in place of the sprawling 'Running From Paradise' or provided a reason to wrestle that track into the three or four minutes that might've better represented it. It's a bit cluttered, which surely could've been resolved in the mix, but there's a soulful lilt and a catchy sing-along chorus that would've made it a nice contrast to the disco-leaning tracks. This could even have been a useful punt as a non-album single: something that wasn't really ever on the H&O radar.

'No Brain, No Pain' (Hall, Sara Allen)

The most punk-influenced song from the *X-Static* sessions turned up as the B-side of 'Wait For Me'. It's not the Pistols or the Ramones you understand – in a British context, it's second or third-division punk: copycat bandwagon-jumping with the obligatory sneering chorus. Probably just something they did in the studio as a bit of a diversion, a bit of fun. Given how few Hall & Oates outtakes have seen release, it's most interesting just to hear them stretch their legs and try something different, even if the result is clichéd.

Above: Looking at ease with their success in 1983. *(Michael Putland)*

Above: Back together again and enjoying themselves. *(Mick Rock)*

Left: Before they settled on 'Daryl Hall & John Oates', they were *Whole Oats*, as this self-titled first album cover says. Witty. *(Atlantic)*

Right: Photographed by Barbara Wilson, the melancholic shot of the Rosedale Diner, left to rot on Route 724, perfectly encapsulates the mood of loss and regret in the title track to *Abandoned Luncheonette*. *(Atlantic)*

Right: An unusually cluttered cover from designer Peter Palombi has everything from Ritz Crackers to baby bottles to presidential campaign badges. *(Atlantic)*

Left: Pierre LaRoche created Bowie's iconic lightning bolt make-up and the famously glamourous reimaging of Daryl and John for their eponymous 'silver' album. *(RCA)*

Left: The second appearance for Ritz Crackers on a Hall & Oates album cover... and just whose sandaled feet are in the bottom of the shot? The enigmatic Sara Allen keeping an eye on things, perhaps? *(RCA)*

Right: Neither professes any love for *Beauty On A Back Street*, though John Beau's photography sharply captures the sleazy darkness of its contents. *(RCA)*

Right: *Along The Red Ledge*, considered by both Daryl and John as one of their very best albums. *(RCA)*

Left: *X-Static*'s eulogising of the portable radio wasn't just in the exuberant track dedicated to it but also in placing one as its cover image. Wasn't modern technology wonderful? *(RCA)*

Left: An early appearance in the UK, for *The Gold Grey Whistle Test*, John taking the lead on 'She's Gone'.

Right: A shocked Daryl relates the story of the 'Maneater'.

Left: At the peak of their powers, Hall & Oates play a Fourth of July benefit gig at New York's Liberty State Park. Hiatus was not far away, though.

Right: John F. Kennedy Stadium, Philadelphia. Live Aid 1985. Hall & Oates provide one of the standout sets of the USA leg. Charlie DeChant and John Oates.

Left: Daryl Hall takes in the enormity of the event.

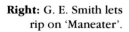

Right: G. E. Smith lets rip on 'Maneater'.

Left and inset: The original cover of *Voices* [pictured] is a striking monochrome concept with soundwaves travelling from John to Daryl. Unusually, subsequent editions [insert] went for a more '80s styling. Dig those purple trousers, John! *(RCA)*

Right: Ed Caraeff, the designer of the *Private Eyes* cover, is most famous for his picture of Hendrix with burning guitar, shot at the 1967 Monterey International Pop Festival. *(RCA)*

Right: Second only to the 'silver' album as their most sexually ambiguous cover image comes *H2O*, shot by Japanese fashion photographer Yasuhiro Wakabayashi. *(RCA)*

Left: The Jackson Pollock stylings of *Big Bam Boom*, conceived by designer Mick Haggerty, set the New York influenced tone of this distinctive album. *(RCA)*

Left: Back
Together Again?
Ooh Yeah! (Arista)

Right: Prudence
Whittlesey's collage
concept for *Change
Of Season* aptly
reflects the album's
sense of Daryl and
John maturing.
(Arista)

Right: They weren't actually walking off into the sunset, but *Marigold Sky* made it seem as if they were. *(Push Records)*

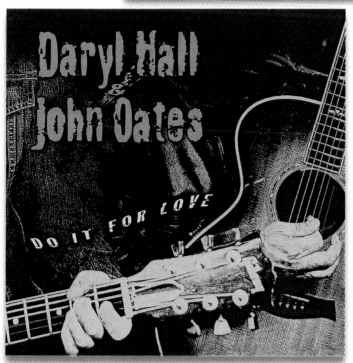

Left: *Do It For Love.* The interior images revealed a moustache-less Oates, not that the cover tells us that. *(U-Watch)*

Above: John Oates affably surveys the scene at Dublin's Olympia Theatre, July 2014, the duo's first appearance in Ireland.

Below: The epitome of the ageing but still cool rock star, Daryl Hall.

Left: Daryl and John play their way through the hits in Dublin.

Left: Dublin Olympia. Only Charlie DeChant remains from the classic Hall & Oates Band (far right of picture), but the players still kick up a storm.

Left: Daryl's first solo album sat on RCA's shelves for three years before being released; Daryl himself looks pragmatic about it. *(RCA)*

Right: *Soul Alone* and soul really matters to him *(Epic)*

Left: The most recent Daryl Hall album. The rather inexplicable title, according to Daryl, represents a state of not knowing what's going on. *(Verve)*

Right: With the legendary moustache long gone, John's craggy and lived-in appearance on the cover of *Mississippi Mile* perfectly complements the maturity of the record. *(PS Records)*

Left: In his later solo records, John has really found his voice away from Hall & Oates, using a great complement of musicians in his Good Road Band. *(PS Records)*

Right: *Arkansas* might be a short record by today's standards, but it's full of heart and love for those musicians who came before. *(PS Records)*

Left: Paying tribute to the songs that influenced their own journey. *(U-Watch)*

Right: Their last studio album to date, *Home For Christmas* is, surprisingly for a holidays record, quite the little gem. *(U-Watch)*

Left: Both Daryl and John considered their gig at the Apollo with Kendrick and Ruffin as a career highlight. *(RCA)*

Voices (1980)

Personnel:
Daryl Hall: vocals, mandar, keyboards, vocoder, synthesizer, percussion
John Oates: vocals, six and twelve-string guitar, percussion
G. E. Smith: guitar
John Siegler: bass
Roger Pope, Jerry Marotta: drums
Chuck Burgi: drums, percussion
Charles DeChant: saxophone
Additional musicians: Jeff Southworth, Ralph Schuckett, Mike Klvana
Recorded at The Hit Factory and Electric Lady Studios, New York
Producers: Daryl Hall, John Oates, Neil Kernon
Release date: 29 July 1980
Label: RCA
Chart Placings: US: 17 UK: -
Running Time: 43:55

Here we go. The 1970s had been a roller coaster of successes, near misses and total failures – a stream of schizophrenic styles that saw Daryl and John traversing genres, trying to find the Hall & Oates sweet spot. In hindsight, *X-Static* signalled their edging up to the new decade with a proper sense of what they wanted to be. Shorn of outside production influences, *Voices* – their first record of the 1980s – set them up with that long-searched-for *voice*. It also opened the floodgates to the commercial success that made them a constant fixture of the charts' upper reaches in the first half of the 1980s, saw them playing on the biggest stages, including a much-lauded performance on the American leg of Live Aid, and acquire them the unfortunate, and untrue, 'mullet and moustachioed sidekick' image that they'd never really be able to shake off. *Voices* also gave them another US No. 1, as well as a blockbuster cover version culled from the LP by another mullet-sporting singer altogether, and finally a slow burn tune that would eventually, in a future digital age, become one of the most streamed songs of all time.

Produced by Hall & Oates with engineer Neil Kernon, *Voices* was recorded over an extended period, with work commencing in November 1979 and being completed the following April. In the process, they visited London again for a two-shows-a-night three-night residency at The Venue in late January before travelling on to Japan for a series of early-February dates.

Looking back, in an interview with *The Sun*, Hall contested that removing an outside producer from the equation was 'extremely important':

If the album had been produced by some of the people that I was working with before, it wouldn't have been as direct or as raw. It would have been creation-by-committee, and that was not what I was about. I didn't want to argue with producers or filter things through other people's perceptions of our music. I was really testing myself as an artist. I was evolving and sucking influences out of the world and trying to combine all those things with my innate Philadelphian-ness.

In a promo radio interview when the album was released, Hall explained:

We had a good idea of what we wanted to do ... this idea of a really raw, basic sound with no overdubs, just rhythm tracks. We decided to use our own voices as the unifying factor, our trademark, what makes us different from everybody else ... The seventies style of music-making was very studio orientated, divorced from live playing, making use of all the new technologies that happened... synthesisers, 24-track sessions, and these different gadgets and technological advances... people made use of everything that came along and it became very overblown. We got caught up in that – I was into a simpler form of statement.

With *Voices* released in July 1980, they swung into action for their most extensive trek to date – a world tour that kicked off in the States through July and August, then moving to the UK in September, finishing the month in Japan. Hopping down for a handful of dates in Australia – where they appeared on the music show *Classic Countdown* – they also flew to New Zealand, then took a short break, seeing out the year with more home dates around New York. In Australia, Don Lane of *The Don Lane Show* described them as 'the Starsky & Hutch of rock 'n' roll' and 'The finest exponents of the Philadelphia sound'. But what's interesting is that at this point, they were still sharing an equal focus, opening their spot on the programme with John's lead on 'How Does It Feel To Be Back', doing the sit-down interview, and resuming with the Daryl-led 'Kiss On My List'. As their visibility grew, the focus would be ever more on the photogenic loved-by-the-camera tall blonde one, and the perception of a sidelined sidekick would grow. But that was still to come.

The album was slow to sell, taking a year to peak. But by then – with its first three singles all making the top 30 in America, the third delivering the smash hit 'Kiss On My List' which hit the top spot in January 1981 – any thoughts of *Voices* being the final H&O album were put aside. They were now ready for the classic three-album run that earned them their place in the roll-call of 1980s pop successes.

'How Does It Feel To Be Back' (Oates)

Oates opens the decade's first H&O album with a stomping track that seems to predict the decade's sound: big, bold, confident and infused with a distinctive – even overblown – production style. It's clear they're building on the direction of *X-Static*, though the production is now largely in their own hands – *Voices* being a marked progression compared to other albums that were largely off on tangents from their immediate predecessor. The track is a nod to new wave, and a little towards AOR. And like other Oates' openers, it's upbeat and passionate with catchy hooks and should've been a hit. As a single, it stalled at number 30, but those stated intentions of being raw and direct are absolutely clear. Oates attributed it to their location: 'Living in New York at the time, you had punk and new wave. We were living in the village. We were in the vortex of all this energy. The music reflected it'.

The song also reflected John's decade-long relationship with model Nancy Hunter (who became his first wife) and the distance between them caused by their separate careers. They'd met at a Minneapolis show: perhaps one at the Orpheum Theatre on 14 or 15 November 1978. John noticed Nancy – a nineteen-year-old college student and confirmed Hall & Oates fan – in the crowd. She later described their meeting: 'We met after the concert. He lived in New York and kept coming back to Minneapolis. I left school and moved to New York. I was quickly signed up by the Ford agency and began a career that took me to shoots all over the world'. First, they bought an apartment in Greenwich Village, and then a farmhouse in Connecticut. 'How Does It Feel To Be Back' reflects the way their work kept them apart: as John described in the sleeve notes for the H&O box set *Do What You Want, Be What You Are*: 'I wrote that thinking about when apart. It was like, 'What would it be like to get back together again?' because we weren't really seeing each other very much'.

'Big Kids' (Hall, Oates)
Remember how back on *Along The Red Ledge* they asked 'Who d'ya think your heroes are?' and came up with the answer 'big kids'? Here's the song that elucidates that apparently throw-away question and answer – a jeans-and-sneakers new-wave pose that could've been a candy-punk Ramones tune if stiffened up and delivered at a more breakneck speed. Others have heard it as akin to Peter Gabriel, Elvis Costello or The Cars, indicating that Hall and Oates had planted themselves firmly in the middle ground between art rock and new wave. *Kulture Kiosk*, in a contextual retrospective, considered this a moment where 'they sang about the present, but kind of foresaw the future, as they lampoon leaders who are really just little emperors in bigger trousers'. They'd come back to this theme again during the 1980s, with 'Adult Education'.

'United State' (Hall, Oates)
This opens with a guitar riff that keeps them firmly in the punk aftermath – a sort of lighter version of a Steve Jones/Sex Pistols entrance salvo, soon to be driven along by Jerry Marotta's busy drumming. There's much to like about the dexterous lyric that sees the protagonist want to 'make an amendment to the constitution/To preserve the state of our union' and ponder 'Do I want to expatriate/Or live in the united state' – mentioning 'inflationary insecurity' and declaiming denial of emotional re-entry. Hall described the song as the duo making a conscious decision to become 'citizens of the world, as opposed to trying to just make it in America. It's about losing that small-thinking patriotism

and looking to a larger thing. Rock 'n' roll is a unifying influence all over the world'. They're both credited here for the lyrics, while the music is all Daryl's, but somebody has sharpened up their lyric-writing skills since the clunky 'totalitarian standards' of 'You Must Be Good For Something'.

'Hard To Be In Love With You' (Hall, Oates, Neal Jason)

On almost any other H&O album, this mid-tempo 'long distance love' soft-rocker would've made a worthy single, a deliciously catchy tune with great harmonies and vocals switching between Daryl on the verses and John on the chorus.

Session player Neal Jason (Brecker Brothers, Meco, Art Garfunkel) co-wrote the music. He told *For Bass Players Only*: 'I think wherever I had been educated and played, I would have eventually gravitated to New York. The amount of clubs in a square city-block in one part of Manhattan ... to get to play live all the time and to meet all the people that gravitate to New York is an advantage to anybody. I immersed myself in the scene and it worked'.

'Kiss On My List' (Hall, Janna Allen)

Here's the monster hit: the duo's first US number one single since 'Rich Girl'. It also introduces new songwriting partner Janna Allen – Sara Allen's younger sister – who'd arrived in New York with the aim of making it as a songwriter and guitarist. Legend has it the song wasn't intended for the album but was simply a demo from the sessions, to give Janna something to use as an example of her work. Remembering it coming 'from left field', John recalled how 'Daryl, as a favour for her, was going to put it down quick in the studio, because it was one of the first songs she'd ever written. He went in with a drum machine and piano and actually recorded the song that way'. Daryl remembered its gestation slightly differently, describing it as the first song he and Janna wrote together:

She had a little Wurlitzer in her apartment in L.A., and we just started writing, literally standing there in a room. She started singing things; it was very much the two of us writing together. We went back to New York and recorded the song as a demo for her on a four-track machine. But everyone loved it so much, we decided to put it on *Voices*.

And it's that demo track, spruced up with background vocals and band additions, including drummer Jerry Marotta's overdub, that got itself on MTV for its very first day of broadcasting. This cemented the 1970s experimental soulsters into the 1980s pop mainstream, in a big way, and on an album that engineer Neil Kernon suggests would've seen the end of the duo had it not been a success: 'The first meeting I had with Daryl and John, John said, 'Neil, just so you know, if this album doesn't do really well, it's probably our last''.

Writing in retrospect for *Stereogum* in 2020, Tom Breihan has a pretty clever view of the song that Hall once described as an anti-love song, saying, 'The whole track feels chintzy and itchy, like the theme to an early-'80s sitcom', and placing it 'somewhere in an uncomfortable zone between slick pseudo-soul '70s and the chirpy style they were in the process of adapting'.

And that anti-love sentiment? Daryl says, 'Everyone thinks it's 'I love you and without you, I would die'. It's the exact opposite of that'.

'Gotta Lotta Nerve (Perfect Perfect)' (Hall, Oates, Sara Allen)

Described by one interviewer as a Carly-Simon-style revenge attitude, Hall replied that he'd been in a nasty mood when he was writing this one, adding that a lot of the words came from Sara Allen.

'You've Lost That Lovin' Feeling' (Phil Spector, Barry Mann, Cynthia Weil)

Describing how the inclusion of this Righteous Brothers classic came as an afterthought at the end of the sessions, Oates recalled a record company album listening party where they concluded something was missing: that the record needed one more song. 'After the party, we went to eat at a local restaurant and that song came on. Went back to the studio and played and recorded it and finished it in one day'. It's such a perfect choice for the album and the duo that it almost feels strange they'd not covered it previously. Released as the album's second single, it did the business: hitting number 12 in *Billboard* in November 1980.

'You Make My Dreams' (Hall, Oates, Sara Allen)

Released as the album's fourth single – after the mighty performance of 'Kiss On My List' – 'You Make My Dreams' reached a respectable number five in the US, and actually peaked at 14 in the UK, bettering the previous single's position there of 33. Since then, it's had success in the streaming era, thanks to appearing in soundtracks like *The Wedding Singer* and *500 Days Of Summer*. Reissued as a Record Store Day pressing in June 2021, the BBC's website said, though 'they're best known in the UK for hits like 'Maneater' and 'I Can't Go For That (No Can Do)', it's 'You Make My Dreams' that's become their most recognisable song'.

Daryl told the BBC: 'What's happened to that song and the way the world embraced it, is absolutely astounding. There's other names on the credits, but I pretty much wrote the song. I started playing that riff on a piano and it just felt good to me'. To *Classic Pop*, he enthused, 'It's crazy how 'You Make My Dreams' has infected the world. And yes, I mean infected rather than affected. There's something so positive about that song'. In September 2020, the *NME* reported on the song reaching a staggering 1,000,000,000 streams, with Oates commenting, 'It's amazing, right? We couldn't have predicted the impact it would have. It's become this anthemic feel-good thing. It took on a life of its own'.

John included a cover of this on his *Mississippi Mile* album, noting it as being 'the odd-ball song on that album. What happened, that was one of those happy accidents, in between takes, in between songs, I'd been fooling around with this kind of Texas swing feel and I sang 'You make my dreams come true' and everyone laughed and said, 'That's cool', so we just cut it and everyone loved it, so it's a little bit of an aberration ... though now I come to think of it, it *is* a song of my youth!'

'Everytime You Go Away' (Hall)

On the 1985 *Live At The Apollo* album – cut with former Temptations David Ruffin and Eddie Kendricks – Daryl introduces this song in a slightly derisory way, recognising the Paul Young cover version that had recently made the top spot on the *Billboard* chart, and peaked at 4 in the UK: 'We'd like to do a song that was on our *Voices* album. It was recently done by an English artist. This is the original, and we're going to do it our own way'. A bit miserly, one might think, given that Hall was enjoying sole publishing on a hugely successful cover of his song on both sides of the Atlantic?

'I heard my very cursory and blunt mention ... but he softened a little after that', Paul Young recalled of that intro, and Daryl does seem to have mellowed, more recently namechecking it when asked about the best H&O cover. 'I always had a soft spot for Paul Young's version of 'Everytime You Go Away', I think he did a great job with that song'.

Having saved the song to a tape of what he described as 'likers', Young almost passed over it in favour of the darker material he'd selected for his *The Secret Of Association* LP, only resurrecting 'Everytime You Go Away' when his manager argued that they needed some lighter tracks.

Young's version is a reinvention of the song, throwing piano, electric sitar, and fretless bass into the mix of what was previously, and ironically given the circumstances of its inclusion to be a lighter entry on *The Secret Of Association,* a much darker number. Shorn of Ralph Schukett's funeral organ that introduces the *Voices* track and which sets the tone for Hall's sombre yet powerful delivery that sits right at the heart of the devastatingly emotional H&O rendition – and, honestly, with Young being a less versatile voice – it flips it into something sprightlier and anthemic, despite the downbeat lyrics. Young had other notable cover version successes, 'Love Of The Common People', and 'Wherever I Lay My Hat (That's My Home)', which gave him a UK number one, but it's this song that has really defined him. 'It's probably the only song I don't get tired of', he once said.

The following year Young duetted with George Michael on the song for a Prince's Trust charity gig, in a performance that also included Elton John, the Marks Knopfler and King, Eric Clapton and Ringo Starr – apparently on the basis that it was the only song on Young's setlist that George Michael knew.

Fast forward a couple of years to September 1988, and you'll find Daryl and John performing a rather extended and chaotic version of the song with none other than The Grateful Dead. Now, that's a strange trip of a different order, man.

'Africa' (Oates)

Not much filler on this largely top-drawer album, but this ill-considered Oates number is definitely out of place, with its tribal drumming, squawky saxophones and talk of how 'My baby went to Africa', where 'She get a couple o' grand and a two-piece suit'. It sounds like John's still worrying himself about Nancy Hunter's modelling career keeping them apart. 'Gotta pack my bags and get to her', he tells us. The listener might be forgiven for wishing he'd just get on and do that very thing.

'Diddy Doo Wop (I Hear The Voices)' (Hall, Oates)

Effectively the album's title track, this is, as Jeff Terich noted in an excellent summation of the song for *Treblezine.com*, 'a song about how a maddening earworm really could cause someone to go on a killing spree ... the lyrics reveal something sinister, even darkly humourous in its subject matter'. Remember how the Son of Sam, David Berkowitz, apparently cited 'Rich Girl' as one of the many bizarre, and frankly unlikely and even disprovable, reasons for his killing spree? Here, emerging out of an insistent regular drum beat and a shrill repeated synthesiser, and juxtaposing the sweet harmonies that deliver the 'diddy doo wop' refrain, is a survey of serial killing music fans. Not just Berkowitz, but also Charles Manson ('Charlie liked The Beatles' – he also very much liked The Beach Boys, but they escape being namechecked here), and the unnamed narrator who has Gene Chandler's classic 1962 chart-topper 'Duke Of Earl' providing the voice in his head. It's a clever piece of work, the catchiness of the song playing against its chilling lyrics. 'The more I think about it' wrote Terich, 'the more fascinated I am by how Hall and Oates not only acknowledged their most notorious fan, they essentially winked back at him'. I'm not convinced that is anything like the case, perhaps it's a cathartic moment of taking back control of this story by the duo. Oates reflected on this in an interview for *The Independent*:

I can't help it if deranged people like our music. We wrote ('Diddy Doo Wop') because at that time, there was a guy riding the subway slashing people. We were wondering what could make somebody so crazy. We thought, you know when you get a song stuck in your head and can't shake it? What if that happens to someone who's mentally imbalanced? What if you had something like 'doo wop' stuck in your head?

So it ends *Voices* on a controversial note, but it also sums up where Daryl and John had arrived at the start of the new decade, building on a style that they'd found with *X-Static* and turning it into a machine that moved them from being, well, hit or miss in the hit parade, to consistently coming up with a sleek run of singles that would keep them in the highest reaches of the charts in the US and beyond, and creating a series of albums that would commercially transcend any of their 1970s output. They'd go on to argue that the continuous stream of 7" successes that 'Kiss On My List' began and begat were themselves a disparate bunch of songs, just as John told me in my interview. 'One thing I'm very proud of is that people mention our string of hits, especially in the '80s, but if you look at those songs you realise that none of them are similar to the other ones'. But at the same time, those songs consolidated not only their most commercial period but stereotyped a view of them that they've found difficult to shake ever since.

Private Eyes (1981)

Personnel:
Daryl Hall: vocals, keyboards, synthesizers, mandar guitar, mandola, mandocella, timbales, CompuRhythm drums
John Oates: vocals, guitar, mando guitar, keyboards
G. E. Smith: lead guitar
Jerry Marotta, Mickey Curry, Chuck Burgi: drums
John Siegler: bass
Charles DeChant: saxophone
Larry Fast: synthesizer, programming
Jeff Southworth, Ray Gomez: guitar
Jimmy Maelen: percussion
John Jarrett: background vocals
Recorded at Electric Lady Studios, New York
Producers: Daryl Hall and John Oates
Release date: 1 September 1981
Label: RCA
Chart Placings: US: 5, UK: 8
Running Time: 47:47

It had all started to happen for them in a big way, and their next LP, *Private Eyes*, was to put those slow-burning *Voices* sales in the shade. 'Kiss On My List' was followed by two more US number ones in the same year: 'Private Eyes' and 'I Can't Go For That (No Can Do)' and while they would never have a UK number one, the latter two were both top ten singles there.

But they came to feel like they were on a roller coaster, in an endless loop of recording, touring and promotional appearances, even being *won* by a school for a performance in a chewing-gum-sponsored competition. Distrustful of the music business generally, they got it down in writing with 'I Can't Go For That', and it would continue to colour their view of the industry for ever more, at turns embracing and rejecting the heady early-1980s days, and seeing their excesses for what they were: mere ephemeral trinkets and accoutrements to the real business of making music. 'We have a realistic view of it', Daryl said.

They were becoming ever more adept at producing themselves, with Neil Kernon engineering and a solid band behind them. 'That's always been our problem. For a long time, every album sounded different', said Daryl. 'Our writing style stayed the same, but each record was a different view of what Hall and Oates should sound like; different producer, different studio musicians. We were having success, but it wasn't the kind of success we wanted. The music just didn't have the edge we wanted it to have ... You don't have to sacrifice intensity in your music in order to have broad appeal. You don't have to make a separation between *pop music* and something that has more guts'.

In a 1981 radio interview, John described their latest working methods:

We worked with home tape recorders this time, more than we've ever done before. We both had four-track cassette machines that you can overdub on. We used them at home to get a better idea, to flesh out a song a little more before we brought it into the studio; colour the song so that when you bring it into the studio, you have a little more specific idea how to deal with it.

Daryl seemed to prefer being on the road:

I really like it. It's completely different from the studio; a time when I don't have to think in the same way. You know where you're going to go because somebody puts you on an aeroplane, so you don't have to think about anything. On stage, we have a set worked out, but within that, there's a lot of room for spontaneity. Our music is very vocal-orientated, so we never do the same thing twice, and the band is tight enough that we can play around with the arrangements. It's very free and unconstricted.

John countered by saying, 'Being on the road is physically exhausting, whereas being in the studio is mentally exhausting'.

Reviewing *Private Eyes* for *Creem* magazine, Richard Riegel said, 'It's a lot like an old Motown album, where all the songs sound pretty much alike and they're all great as a consequence'. He seemed particularly – if rather sarcastically – pleased that they'd found the sweet spot that he felt had eluded them all these years: 'I realise that Rev. Gamble and Prof. Rundgren tried to keep it a secret from you, but it's a fact that all that great black soul music of the '60s was chock full of beat and rhythm and drive. Glad you finally discovered all that stuff in your own music'.

'Private Eyes' (Hall, Warren Pash, Sara Allen, Janna Allen)
In a way, 'Private Eyes' was as much happenstance as the earlier Janna Allen co-write 'Kiss On My List'. Warren Pash was a Los Angeles-based musician playing in a band called The Cheaters. He met Daryl and Janna at an L.A. Cheaters gig in early 1980 and began working on some songs with Daryl in a loose, informal way. Warren told *Songwriter.com*: 'He would throw some ideas at me and see if I could come up with anything, and nothing was really sticking, but he kept trying'. One of the songs Pash was working on – seemingly outside of his writing with Hall – was called 'I Need You To Need Me', which became 'Private Eyes' after Pash spotted a *Billboard* for the film *The Private Eyes*. This led to a session with Janna, who was pursuing a singing career and passed the tape on to Daryl on the basis he'd know how to develop the song properly.

Though the duo always made a thing about their singles all being different from each other, there's a definite case to be made for 'Private Eyes' being

'Kiss On My List II'. It has the same piano sound driving a feel-good vibe with a darker undertone in the lyrics, as though they'd spotted a formula to go with for the first time.

Picked as the title track for the follow-up to *Voices,* it's the epitome of the much-maligned sound of the first years of the 1980s. It has a big sound, irritating handclaps, slightly off-colour (in retrospect) lyrics (see most notably 'Every Breath You Take' by The Police), and an easy sing-a-long chorus. But it's great, full of confidence and purpose and pretty much unforgettable from the intro onwards. Their long-time collaborator Tom T-Bone Wolk, hired the night before the very literal promo film was made, makes his debut on bass for the video – though not on the track itself – a stood-still figure in trench coat and hat who judiciously avoids the communal handclapping that punctuates the song. According to radio promos, he'd asked, 'what do I do?' and Hall replied, 'you just be the guy who stands there.' So, he did.

'Looking For A Good Sign' (Hall)
This is dedicated to David, Eddie, Melvin, Otis and Paul – not (as some note) the original Temptations, but their classic 'My Girl' line-up when David Ruffin replaced founder-member Elbridge Bryant – and their influence permeates this Motown-tinged number. That admiration culminated in Ruffin and Eddie Kendricks joining H&O for their 1985 US Live Aid appearance, and the album *Live At The Apollo* released two months later. Daryl recalled: 'They were an outrageous influence on me. After (their shows), they would just go and sing gospel songs and stuff. I felt that was something I belonged doing'. Another time, he noted how 'I don't see any distinction between black and white music. I grew up in a very mixed-raced environment. My singing style came from that'. He claimed to have actually dreamed this song, and had to quickly sing it into his tape recorder upon waking up. He said at the time: 'It's one of the most perfectly constructed songs we've ever done. The arrangement, you rarely get it just right, but that song, it's a piece of nostalgia'.

'I Can't Go For That (No Can Do)' (Hall, Oates, Sara Allen)
On this shiny slick dancefloor filler, Hall gives a broad hint of a relationship gone stale:

I can't go for being twice as nice
I can't go for just repeating the same old lines

'Most people think the song is about a relationship and it is,' Hall told The Guardian in 2018, 'but one with the music industry. I felt very manipulated'. And Oates added, 'I actually regret not saying 'No can do' to more things – like the Learjet race for MTV. Daryl started on the east coast, I was on the west, and we each got in a Learjet with some fans and had a race to Oklahoma. It was the '80s ... everything was oversized, excessive and ridiculous'. Another time, Hall would contest that 'I exist in spite of the music business. The music business never did me any favours'.

It's most definitely a song of the 1980s in its clean production sheen, even though the decade was still young, Hall wrote the music from experimenting with the Roland CR-78 drum machine he'd used for 'Kiss On My List'. The machine had been around since 1978 and was starting to become ubiquitous, having featured on the Phil Collins hit 'In The Air Tonight' just months before. Using the Rock 1 pre-set, Hall described to *Mix* how he 'sat down at a Korg organ and started to play this bass line that was coming to me. The chords came together and I heard a guitar riff, which I asked John to play. I wrote most of the lyrics, but Sara contributed some ideas'. In live shows, it became an extended piece, with Hall letting his vocal flow, but less successfully turning the middle-eight into a rather awkward rap section: 'There comes a time/When you gotta draw the line/You can't do this/You can't do that/You gotta put your foot down'. No should do, Daryl.

But while rooted to its time it be might be, it's still a great tune. And though it could be something of an albatross with its success and familiarity tagging H&O with a particular smoothness from which much of the 'yacht rock' epithet derives, the fact it doesn't overpower their other hit records says much about about the distinctness of their singles. As John told this writer: 'We never fell into the trap of 'We've had this big number one, let's make the sequel''. He recalled this song being cited by Michael Jackson as an inspiration, telling *The Independent* that at Live Aid 'Michael Jackson came up to us backstage. He said he loved to dance to 'I Can't Go For That', and it had inspired the bass line for 'Billie Jean'. Hall, in turn, remembered his own response as simply, 'Oh Michael, what do I care? You did it very differently'.

'Mano A Mano' (Oates)
The lyric of this infectious Oates number is typical of the moral fibre that can often be found running through his songs, with its appeal to just get on with each other and set a positive example as 'the hand that rocks the cradle'. It might be a lesser-known H&O song, but with its simple and direct message, catchy stuttering chorus and delicious G. E. Smith guitar lick in its middle eight, it's a top-drawer album cut. John said, 'It's a perversion of the phrase hand-to-hand. It's meant to represent hand-to-hand combat, but I made it a universal love song'.

'Did It In A Minute' (Hall, Sara Allen, Janna Allen)
Though both Allen sisters are credited alongside Daryl for the writing, this sounds for all the world like 'Kiss On My List' revisited, suggesting Janna's influence here was the stronger of the three. Some hear the reliance on the 'you did it, you did it, you did it' refrain as being borrowed from Eric Carmen's 1977 hit 'She Did It', itself inspired by The Beach Boys' 'Do It Again'.

A weaker link on an album where there's arguably no filler, this frantic tale of the fizz of finding love at first sight, peaked at number nine, a minor disappointment after the album's two chart-toppers, but respectable in its own right and, really, this one is great or grating depending on how the listener hears that refrain.

'Head Above Water' (Hall, Oates, Sara Allen)

Reviewing in 2007, Michael R. Smith on *The Daily Vault* bemoaned 'Head Above Water' as having the 'annoying plunking sound of an electric piano' and thought it sounded 'like a rejected track by Survivor'. What? That plunking keyboard sound hadn't done too badly for Benny Andersson on ABBA's 'Dancing Queen', or for Steve Nieve on Elvis Costello's 'Oliver's Army', and it does alright for Daryl Hall here. This is the album's most muscular track – there's nothing wrong with a change of pace and texture – with Mickey Curry booming and clattering around the drum kit, and John Siegler's pensive bass lines combined with that electric piano which keeps this one nicely busy. Lyrically, it's probably a companion piece to 'I Can't Go For That (No Can Do)', in relentlessly describing how difficult just keeping going in the music industry can be, and is a reminder to go your own way and 'Never envy the big fish in da pond'. *Private Eyes* was even more of a breakthrough career-defining album than *Voices*, and after ten years of hits and misses, Daryl and John were finding them*selves* becoming the big fish.

'Tell Me What You Want' (Hall, Sara Allen)

This starts with a muted extract from Hall's initial home demo – where he's playing with words, with the shape of words, and working the song out – and a background ticking-clock effect that works alongside Jerry Marotta's metronomic drumming throughout. But the track is a little bit less than that intriguing start suggests it's going to be, as if it never really developed beyond that initial demo.

'Friday Let Me Down' (Hall, Oates, Sara Allen)

Here's a nice example of the unrequited love song's sub-genre: the telephone call with no reply. Better known examples are certainly Jack Lee's 'Hanging On The Telephone' (made famous by Blondie), ELO's 'Telephone Line' and Dr Hook's valiant attempts to bypass the phone-hogging 'Sylvia's Mother', but 'Friday Let Me Down' is a worthy entry nonetheless. Not so much a call and response tune, more a call and no response saga, always with the rather cold, and ultimately unrealised promise that if the caller leaves his name on the answer machine, 'I will call you Friday night. Call you Friday, goodbye'. Its circularity is quite engaging, always relentlessly returning to the disappointment that inevitably comes when the tape machine is once again the only voice on the other end of the phone.

Asked about possibly dusting off 'Friday Let Me Down' for his solo sets, John thought it unlikely. 'That's kind of a production, you know? A little tough sometimes. Some of the songs that are a little more rooted in production, don't translate as well'. But tracks such as this, 'Head Above Water' and 'Mano A Mano', bind the album outside its two big hitters, and though that production John mentions is very much of its day, these tracks have stood the test of time much better than others among their contemporaries.

'Unguarded Minute' (Hall, Oates, Sara Allen)
Though John must have some words in the lyrics here – the music is all Daryl – 'Unguarded Minute' is a typical Hall and Allen angsty, relationship teetering on the brink, should have done things differently, trying to define roles, song.

'Your Imagination' (Hall)
While during his marriage to Nancy Hunter, John would write songs reflecting his own paranoias about being apart in different time zones or countries, here Daryl gives quite the opposite viewpoint. It's about a needy, jealous lover who is unpicking every word and letting their imagination run riot as to what he's up to – though it suggests a lack of empathy when he claims he's doing 'nothing you could really say is wrong', placing any perceived misdemeanours as being a matter of perspective.

Interesting to see the differences in approach between Daryl and John's writings as displayed in songs that are ostensibly around the same hang-ups and fears. And that squares to how they are perceived as people, as co-producer Neil Kernon summed them up in an interview for *MelodicRock.com*:

Daryl is the type that gets antsy, smokes a lot; can't-sit-still type. John, on the other hand, is very thorough, keeps his feet on the ground, and generally provides the stability for their relationship. I think it's fair to say that they have always seemed to do much better when they worked together than when they worked separately.

'Some Men' (Hall)
This is just the kind of song Neil Kernon reckoned he'd originally been approached to help with, based on what Tommy Mottola had told him: 'Daryl and John were looking for someone who made punchy hard-edged records. I had been making punk and new wave records, and Daryl was really into all that'. 'Some Men' is a febrile and frenetic album closer, with verbose, sprawling lyrics and forthright lead guitar, ending *Private Eyes* with a riotous playout and heading for a 1981 Grammy nomination for 'Best Pop Vocal Performance by a Duo or Group with Vocal'. They'd also get nominated the following year in the same category for their 'Maneater' single.

H2O (1982)

Personnel:
Daryl Hall: vocals, keyboards, synthesizer, guitar
John Oates: vocals, six and twelve-string guitar, electric piano, CompuRhythm drums
G. E. Smith: lead guitar
Mickey Curry: drums
Tom T. Bone Wolk: bass
Charles DeChant: saxophone
Larry Fast: synthesizer programming
Recorded at Electric Lady Studios, New York
Producers: Daryl Hall, John Oates, Neil Kernon
Release date: 4 October 1982
Label: RCA
Chart Placings: US: 3, UK: 24
Running Time: 47:08

Now we've arrived at peak Hall & Oates: on top of their game and at their most easily-caricatured point. This is the era most casual listeners would think of when they hear Daryl and John's names – the 'Maneater' bass intro; Daryl's flowing mullet hairstyle; their take on Mike Oldfield's 'Family Man'; the are-they/aren't-they sexual ambiguity, and that moustache. They were battling media-stereotyping, with journalists simply wanting to pigeonhole them as the dominant lead singer and his trusty guitar-playing sidekick, and characterise them as an American equivalent to the newly-emerged UK duo Wham!. It was completely lazy, mattering not that Oates was writing some of their best material – far better for the sake of points scoring in the press to set up Oates as Hall's very own Andrew Ridgley, particularly with G. E. Smith and Tom Wolk taking most of the lead guitar. All arrant nonsense, of course. But for right-on purist music journalists still coming off the back of punk rock, H&O were such an easy target.

Writing for *NME* in November 1982, Richard Cook suggested that though the duo's British profile had only slightly increased (which frankly is hard to square with *Private Eyes'* UK top ten success), 'The sudden onrush of Hall and Oates into the centre-stage of American music was – along with the extraordinary revitalisation of the J. Geils Band – the most remarkable Stateside resurgence of last year. [It] at a stroke, re-grooved two veterans into a look they'd modelled ten years before: The Acceptable Sound of Young America'. In response, John thought that 'Radio in America's in synch with us now. Instead of us trying to jam things down their throat, we're a benchmark of what pop is in America'.

But asked on *American Bandstand* if, at the height of their popularity, they worried about the hits drying up, John replied, 'I don't know anything about hit records. We just make the best records we can, and if they're hits, then great'. They were pragmatic about the point they'd arrived at. Pressed on whether they were prepared for a day their current success proved fleeting, Daryl said, 'We'd like to think that we are, but you're never really prepared for it. We make music for other reasons. We want to make a lot of money, sure, that's fun. But we've been making music most of our lives, and the commercial success is great, but it's not the only thing we're working for'.

As it transpired, that day of reckoning wasn't far away, even though they had another big album to come. But at this point, *H20* was capturing the musical zeitgeist: a tempting confection of their beloved soul dipped in a melting pot of synth-pop played in a hard-edged style, with the definitive Hall & Oates band now including the newly-arrived Tom Wolk, who'd become a vital component of the lineup they'd been searching for.

Trade journal *Billboard* was soon to describe them as the most successful duo of all time, though Daryl claimed to be uncomfortable with that: 'I feel a little strange about that ... we're not so much a duo as a songwriting team that fronts a band. We're nothing like Simon & Garfunkel. Rather, we're more like a Lennon & McCartney'. That made a lot of sense given the creative machinery of the H&O concept, not just with additional writing partners, but in the way that Tom Wolk came to be a key figure – almost a partner who made them a trio in all but name – and from the sonic and stage presence of someone such as Charles DeChant. They were known and categorised as a duo, but that was never really it, and *H2O* was very much the epitome of that, with the Allen sisters and the Hall & Oates band right at the core.

'Maneater' (Hall, Oates, Sara Allen)

Irresistibly infectious bass lines, bubbly keyboards and that great smoky nighttime saxophone middle eight. Watch out, here it comes, it's the 'Maneater' of much repute: very much of its decade and still timeless. 'We were both notoriously bad at picking singles,' Oates recalled, 'but that one leapt out'. It also leapt up the US charts for a four-week stay in the number one slot: their fifth time at the top and their longest stint there. 'It captures a mood of New York in the 1980s. Lean, sparse, edgy, new-wave-meets-pop. Perfectly suited for the time'.

John further expanded to the *Philadelphia Enquirer*: 'It's about greed, avarice and spoiled riches. But we have it in the setting of a girl because it's more relatable. That's what we do all of the time'. In the *New York Post*, he described its genesis as coming from 'a beautiful girl who swore like a sailor. The juxtaposition was too good to resist. I thought, 'Man, she would chew you up and spit you out'. But it's really a metaphor for New York City in the '80s. The 'Maneater' is the city itself'.

In a rare interview for *Smash Hits* in 1983, Sara Allen noted, 'We were terrified of getting too mellow ... but a quick trip to New York soon changes that'. Daryl later credited her with refining the song they already had, which had switched from its original vague reggae to what he described to *American Songwriter* as a 'Motown kind of groove'. The original lyric added a sequence of other monikers following on from the 'maneater' tag: '(Sara) said, 'Drop that shit in the end, and go 'She's a maneater' and stop!'. I thought about it and realised she was right. It made all the difference'.

While it might be the bouncy bass and Hall's admonishing vocals that are the song's signature hooks, Charlie DeChant's saxophone is the other key component, having already cemented itself via songs like 'I Can't Go For That (No Can Do)' as a key part of the overall H&O sound. Hall said, 'I'm sorry that the saxophone solo went away, but everything comes back. It's a very expressive instrument. It's as close to a voice as any instrument I can think of'.

'Crime Pays' (Hall, Oates, Sara Allen)
A lyrical counterpoint to 'Private Eyes' and a hint towards how the duo's sound would develop on their next album *Big Bam Boom*, 'Crime Pays' abandons their beloved Philadelphia feel for a move into Prince territory with a funk rock, Minneapolis sound. Talking to *NME* in 2020, Oates claimed, 'We were one of the first real crossover artists. We were getting played on both R&B radio *and* pop radio before Prince etc., and I think opening those doors and breaking down racial barriers is something we don't get enough credit for'. A British music press inkie from back in the day claimed in one feature that Daryl and John had more soul in their little fingers than Prince had in his entire body... a huge exaggeration and one that the writer surely repented on at leisure, but a nugget of thinking placing them within a pantheon nonetheless, and 'Crime Pays' inarguably locks into a Prince groove with aplomb.

It also sounds like another stepping stone in their quest to combine disparate influences – what came from blue-eyed soul, stretching out to reflect the whole melting pot of things and people around them. Daryl reflected in a *Smash Hits* interview:

> We live in a city, and all kinds of people live there together. If you're going to reflect that honestly, you've got to have an integrated style. There are a lot of ethnic combinations in the city: black, Puerto Rican, Italian, whatever you are. It's (what) rock and roll was in the beginning with its mixture of black and white music. We started in that tradition. We grew up in the '60s, and we played with black and white groups. That's why we call our music rock and soul. We want to be ambassadors!'

'Art Of Heartbreak' (Hall, Janna Allen, Sara Allen)
This shows the last throes of a toxic relationship where 'We kiss and we hiss at the same time'. It's an understated gem, made complete by the self-styled Mr. Casual's elegantly smooth saxophone creating something akin to a theme tune each time the song title appears. It's credited as a Janna Allen composition with Daryl and Sara chipping in with lyrics. Through that sax, however, Charlie DeChant is the mournful heart at the centre of what comes across as a genuinely regretful lament. From early promo material, it seems this came in as

a late replacement for a track called 'Thin Ice': thought to be a Hall/Allen-sisters song in the vein of the album's 'Guessing Games'.

'One On One' (Hall)
Another smoochy smooth classic, in the vein of 'Sara Smile' to a degree, 'One On One' followed 'Maneater' as the album's second single, reaching a very respectable seven in the US, but having a strangely muted presence in the UK charts, where it stalled well outside the Top 50.

On the face of it, it reads as a world-weary plea for some space, private time and intimacy that's been missing; finding the moment where 'There's nothing else but you and me'. But being a Hall song, what's on the surface isn't quite what's underneath, and it's less about emotional connection than dissatisfaction and a need for change and renewal. As Oates once said, 'Our songs are deceptively simple, but I think if you delve deeper, there's more going on'.

This is all Daryl, deploying a silky, restrained vocal, and taking a basketball metaphor leading to the track being adopted for NBA promos in the 1980s. He described it to *Entertainment Weekly* as a reflection of the rootless way of life he'd experienced as a musician: 'I was on the road, living this very transient life. You're everywhere and you're nowhere, and your domestic life – your concept of home – becomes very special. This song sort of describes that'.

'Open All Night' (Hall, Sara Allen)
Very interestingly positioned at the end of the album's first side, given that flipping over to the second takes us into the notorious subject matter of 'Family Man', the dark discovery of serial infidelity displayed heart-on-sleeve can be taken as being as heavy in its betrayal as the listener wants to imagine it. It's the uncovering of a workplace affair that continued after hours, or the realisation that the protagonist's partner has been 'selling favours' while he was out of town. It has a very affecting Daryl/John counterplay – 'Don't ask me to tell you', 'No I don't wanna tell you' – with a Hall vocal articulating the narrator's anguish at the discovery.

'Family Man' (Tim Cross, Rick Fenn, Mike Frye, Mike Oldfield, Morris Pert, Maggie Reilly)
This is both a cover of the Mike Oldfield and Maggie Reilly song of a self-declared family man's attempted solicitation by a prostitute, and a lyrical rethinking of the tale's denouement. Oldfield cut it for his *Five Miles Out* album, a moderate success when picked as a single, reaching No. 45 in the UK, a curious case of electronic minimalism leading into a strangely sparse-yet-cluttered pop tune. Daryl and John reconceive it as a soft rocker with a much more commercial posturing (including a delicious G. E. Smith lead break) which took it thirty places higher than Oldfield's version in the UK and to No. 6 in the US even if perhaps it loses the sleazy grit of the original.

In Oldfield's version, there's a clear boundary, however, the woman pressing her services on four instances and being aggressively rebuffed, and while there's a midpoint where the man concedes that 'if you push me too far, I just might', Daryl and John's version push the scenario further, ending on an uncredited new verse that says the family man had actually decided to acquire these services, that it was mostly a matter of building up courage, but in getting to that point has left it too late and the woman has left in search of another target. Probably in self-justification, he screams out the 'leave me alone...' chorus as the song ends.

It's almost the opposite of 'Everytime You Go Away'. Where Paul Young's cover of that song is recognised as definitive to the extent that many are surprised to discover it's actually a Hall & Oates song, 'Family Man' has become so inextricably linked with them that it has largely obscured the Oldfield version.

'Italian Girls' (Oates)

Here's Oates visiting Rome and anticipating the 'Hollywood on the Tiber' of *Quo Vadis*, *Roman Holiday*, the Sophia Loren vehicles *Boy On A Dolphin* and *It Started In Naples*, and the hedonism of *La Dolce Vita*. Of course, life doesn't always reflect art, as we know, and he's left disappointed when he discovers ancient ruins, great Italian art, more pasta than he can eat... but none of those wonderful leading ladies. Despite that, he takes it all in good spirits, in this sprightly grin-inducing sing-along. With a wealth of strong single A-side candidates, this song missed its chance, except in Canada for some reason, but there surely must be a parallel world somewhere in which 'Italian Girls' was a successful bit of summer fluff for the singles chart. As Oates told this author: "'Italian Girls' was very strange. I was on my first trip to Italy and with this image in my head of the classic Italian movies and the beautiful women who were associated with those movies. I thought I'd go there and fall in love and have this great Italian experience ... and nothing happened! So, I can come from the most profound inspiration to the most...'

'Guessing Games' (Hall, Janna Allen)

By this point, we've heard the album's famous songs, those tracks that, culled as singles, became key components of the live set, and it's tempting to think the album is running out of steam, a notion that the syrupy-sweet, and very much Hall-&-Oates-by-numbers, 'Guessing Games' doesn't particularly dispel, even though many fans rate this one, like 'Italian Girls', as a single that should've been. It's pretty much as *NME*'s Leyla Sanai described in her undeserved hatchet job: 'No sting, no bite ... kissing the light, airy touch goodbye ... nice bass here, strong chorus there, decent note on the trumpet, good thump on the drum. (But) by the time analysis is over, the hot bits have gone tepid and the rest has congealed'. Sanai was absolutely not right, overall, but 'Guessing Games' has more than a bit of what the review is getting at, pleasant as it might well be.

'Delayed Reaction' (Hall, Oates, Sara Allen)

One of the album's most straightforward rock numbers from its ascending and scene-setting guitar riff onwards, this almost feels like it comes from the Nick Lowe/Ducks Deluxe 1970s British pub rock scene, just a bit delayed out of the blocks. Perhaps that *was* an influence since Hall and Lowe became friends later in the decade, Hall recalling to Ken Sharp how 'We got together in England and wrote a song called 'When The Spell Is Broken'. I still love that song and eventually, I'm going to record it. We've maintained a friendship'. As a side note here, in 2012, Daryl, Lowe and T-Bone Wolk played a great acoustic rendition of Lowe's 'Cruel To Be Kind' on an episode of Hall's *Live From Daryl's House* internet show that's worth searching out.

'At Tension' (Oates)

Now the album is really starting to fizzle out. Clocking in at over six minutes, this Oates number is plodding, uninspired, slow-moving and sounding like filler that outstays its welcome. He's playing with army themes, punning on 'standing at tension' in place of 'attention' on a track that's much more experimental in its way than we're used to hearing from him, but it's not a patch on the joyous 'Italian Girls' and makes you feel like it's been added to give John a second chunk of solo publishing on the album.

'Go Solo' (Hall)

'Go Solo' feels less like a breakup song and more like Daryl ruminating on his next move – prescient or plan forming, given the way he and John would drift apart after the following LP, as though he's urging himself onwards: 'Play a brand new part/Go solo, solo'. Looking back in 2007 for *Pitchfork*, he claimed, 'We are not an equal duo, and never have been. I'm ninety percent and he's ten percent, and that's the way it is. He has plenty of ideas; he's a finisher, a good musician, he's overshadowed by me because I'm such a strong vocal personality'. But he qualified it with 'He's my brother. A very, very talented person'.

John's expressed his view to *NME*: 'Because of Daryl's incredible talent, people think I don't do anything'. He confessed this had worried him over the years, 'but at the same time, I'm comfortable in my own skin and know what I bring to the table'. But the way the final *H2O* tracks indicated a divided vision developing, signposted the duo's future.

Related Tracks

'Jingle Bell Rock' (Joe Beal, Jim Boothe)

This non-album double-A-side cover of the 1957 Bobby Helms holiday classic – with Daryl's vocal on the A-side and John's getting almost parity on the flip – is quite a curiosity. Many years later, they'd go the whole, umm, turkey, and release a Christmas/Holidays album, but this one came with a cheesy Christmas video where Daryl and John are presented almost as a wholesome 1950s-style All-American family, welcoming in friends laden down with gifts and refusing entrance to an altogether more raucous bunch of carol singers. It's a bit of fun and nonsense, let's leave it there...

'Say It Isn't So (Hall)

The traditional one-a-year studio album failed to materialise in 1983. In its place appeared the first Hall & Oates compilation since *No Goodbyes* in 1977 (though RCA had released *The Hall & Oates Collection* in Australia and New Zealand in 1981). *Rock 'n' Soul Part 1* (don't go looking for *Part 2*, it doesn't exist) rounded up the most successful RCA-era singles to date, adding 'She's Gone' from the Atlantic days, and two new singles – 'Adult Education' and 'Say It Isn't So' – cut at Electric Lady studios in September 1983.

In 2015, the duo sued Early Bird Foods for their Haulin' Oats granola branding. 'Say It Isn't So' tweeted Early Bird in response – cue other responses of how the duo 'can't go for that' - which is probably the most interesting thing that can be noted of this much-loved but blandly super smooth song.

'Adult Education' (Hall, Oates, Sara Allen)

It's not unusual for pop and rock songs to strike a pose and disparage education and learning. Bruce Springsteen famously sang in 'No Surrender' of how he and his unnamed blood brother took their education from a three-minute record, and it surpassed anything they'd learned in school, while in The Specials' 'Rat Race', singer Terry Hall complained about the lack of benefit derived from his solitary art O Level (a 1980s British senior-school qualification). 'Adult Education' doesn't quite follow those lines, but it's still a message to the student body – beset with their traditional hang-ups and issues – that there's life after high school, and that's where they'll start to grow up and properly learn things. Daryl has claimed it largely as his own song, noting that John chipped in a line, but he couldn't recall Sara's contribution.

Then there's the Tim Pope video. Well, if you think back to the video for 'She's Gone', directed by John's sister and made on pretty much a shoestring budget, here's the evidence that money doesn't necessarily do better. In a fiery Indiana Jones or even post-apocalypse temple setting, Hall croons along while Oates looks sheepish, and neither seems to have a clue what's going on or if there is any plot whatsoever to the proceedings – if there is, it has nothing to do with the lyrics, anyway.

Big Bam Boom (1984)

Personnel:
Daryl Hall: vocals, synthesizer, guitar
John Oates: vocals, guitar, synth-guitar, synthesizers
G. E. Smith: lead guitar
Tom 'T-Bone' Wolk: bass, synthesizer, guitar
Mickey Curry: drums
Charlie DeChant: saxophone
Recorded at Electric Lady Studio
Producers: Daryl Hall, John Oates, Bob Clearmountain
Release date: 12 October 1984
Label: RCA
Chart Placings: US: 5, UK: 28
Running Time: 40:13

I asked John Oates which albums he saw as being the key moments in the Hall & Oates catalogue:

> I can give them to you; I've thought about this a lot actually. I think there are very specific albums that represent an important change or moment. The first would be Abandoned Luncheonette, the next would be *Along The Red Ledge,* the next *Voices,* because that was when we started producing ourselves. The next I'd say was *Big Bam Boom* because it's so experimental and is our transition from the analogue to digital worlds. And that's it, right there. That set the course for the rest of our lives and career.

With a run of three career-defining albums that are almost a trilogy – not connected by concept, but by an audible refinement of sound and style – the duo took some downtime. They'd been busy touring North America until August 1983, then recording the two new songs for *Rock 'N Soul Part 1*, letting that compilation serve as the year's main offering, only surfacing again with the 'Jingle Bell Rock' Christmas single. The early months of 1984 saw them on a substantial run of international dates in Australia, Thailand, Japan and Europe, including major shows in the UK – playing three nights at Wembley Arena and another at Birmingham's NEC – before starting work on their next album *Big Bam Boom*.

Catching them at Wembley, *Melody Maker*'s Adam Sweeting spotted the way Oates' stage profile was diminishing: 'A little more of Oates would have lent some variety. The pair's duo on 'Lovin' Feeling' was a showstopper, while Oates' lead on the fluently poppy 'Italian Girls' proved a viable alternative to Hall's more extravagant notions of self-presentation'.

Despite their insistence on the benefits of self-production, after the fractious end to their relationship with Christopher Bond – and David Foster's realisation that he was becoming a conduit for their production ideas rather than his own – they'd never properly let go of third-party production, with Neil Kernon working with them on what could loosely be described as their RCA phase II. On *Big Bam Boom* they'd have Bob Clearmountain engineering and mixing them, but also credited as a co-producer, who'd also engineer and mix *Born In The USA* the same year, and, with surely an eye on the burgeoning 12" remix market, hook-up with Arthur Baker, the point-man in DJ remixes of the moment, the 'Mix Master General' as Daryl would put it. What it delivered was music that most reflected their notion of being about the city; of reflecting New York in all its multi-faceted glory. They used cutting-edge technology unimaginable back when they thought their use of the Roland drum machine to be pioneering, and adopted the use of found sounds to populate the background to their soundtrack.

Big Bam Boom should've been the pinnacle, the cherry on top of their run of commercial smashes, and it is still a dynamic and vivid urban capture, just as they intended. Its US peak of 5 equalled *Private Eyes* and only eased them a couple of spots lower than *H2O*. But for all the envelope-pushing and experimentation, and for as much as they continued to rate *Big Bam Boom* as a particular high point, it crystallised just as their momentum was stalling and they began to display some fraying at the edges.

That possibly came from their profile reaching levels they'd perhaps never anticipated, with their distrust of music business trappings having been obvious as far back as the *War Babies* concept. Now they were in the big time, with its ostentatious trappings. In the emerging corporatisation of rock music, sponsor General Motors used their mid-range sports car – the rather unloved Pontiac Fiero – as the headlining mascot for the *Big Bam Boom* tour. It's no wonder then that when you revisit features such as Lynn Hirschberg's January-1985 *Rolling Stone* piece 'Hall and Oates: The Self-Righteous Brothers', the sense of it all unravelling – even without the rancour that some other acts descended into – is evident.

Lynn Hirschberg – having been present at a live H&O MTV appearance – describes in that *Rolling Stone* piece the disinterest and weariness present in the duo's answers to fan questions. Viewing the show on YouTube is truly as painful as her piece suggests, because – notwithstanding that it's a largely young fan audience calling in, with the natural awkwardness and lack of sophistication that entails – the responses come across as bored and curt: Daryl playing around with a cigarette packet as if his disinterest required a bit more signalling. In its defence, it's stagy and painful in any case, far too long, and with cuts to phone questions that have nobody on the line, and multiple callers who only want to talk to Daryl. But it's still indicative of a particular mood that appears to have fallen on them.

Q: 'I'm calling from Kansas City, Missouri [clearly nervous]. How did you get started?'.
Daryl: 'We met in school. That's how we got started'.

[The interviewer Mark Goodman expands, but with an exasperated 'I'm not supposed to tell the story...'.]

Q: 'What would Daryl and John be doing if they weren't musicians?'.
Both, not disguising the tedium: 'Good question. Good question. Good question. Looking for a job'.

Q: 'I'd like to ask Daryl Hall what his favourite group is?'.
Daryl, unhelpfully: 'The Three Stooges'.
Mark Goodman, trying to cover and make it about both musicians: 'John, you got a favourite group?'
John: 'No'.

Hirschberg sums it up: '[Daryl] is clearly miserable. Oates is clearly miserable. Even Mark Goodman, hosting this phone-in to promote the duo's new album, is clearly miserable. Tommy Mottola scurries about the soundstage. 'Do we have people ready to call with better questions?'. Calls are coming in rapidly, but the questions are no good'. Hirschberg reflects that Daryl and John – still living near each other in Greenwich Village – 'don't socialise together much. Hall pals around with actors Mickey Rourke and Sean Penn. Oates spends a lot of time with his wife, Nancy. They've become the most successful duo in music history by combining art with business, balancing the two extremes for the last fifteen years'. She identifies what she saw as the cracks that had developed in the H&O setup, just as Adam Sweeting had in his Wembley Arena review the prior year: 'Daryl Hall is the star. Oates is, technically speaking, an equal partner, but Hall writes most of the songs, performs most of the songs and dominates their videos and concerts. The two have a strange relationship. Hall doesn't seem to really like Oates, and Oates seems removed, even distant from the entire Hall and Oates organisation. But they're both professionals'. It's a piece totally based on the schisms the writer perceives to have developed between them – not insurmountable, but fifteen years on, probably worthy of some sort of break.

By this point, of course, they'd become fair game for music press disdain. *Musician* magazine's Roy Trakin viewed *Big Bam Boom* positively in places, but looked for negatives in others: 'The nagging thought remains that there's a void at the heart of H&O's music that ultimately makes their soul sound ersatz. Could it be that the twosome's pinup looks, overshadow their own skills, making their sound seem more styled than substantive?'. But he also considered that while the album 'may not win over all their critics with its savvy appropriation of street credibility, it will certainly do nothing to brake [sic] their popular momentum'.

Big Bam Boom was the point at which their endless cycle of recording and touring, temporarily paused. Unfortunately, it also reflected in sales; a jumping-off point for some fans, most probably.

'Dance On Your Knees' (Hall, Arthur Baker)

From its opening synthesiser note, into the energetic drum patterns and bassline, the arrival of the guitar riff and the treated voices, attacking and sprawling like the Jackson Pollock inspired splatter of the cover art, it's clear that our duo have moved their sound onward in a distinctly urban, cutting-edge tech, direction. Sharp and to the point and ending on that titular instruction... 'dance on your knees!'

'Sampling and digital technology was coming into its own', recalled Oates in the notes for the 2004 reissue. 'We tried to be as experimental as we could and at the same time be commercially successful. Digital tape recorders, digital sampling ... we absorbed it: Synclaviers, Fairlights, all these new digital keyboards. We recorded on analog tape [but] it was a hybrid at the end of the digital era and the beginning of digital'.

It's a dance track of a sort they'd never attempted before, positioning them in a scene that hadn't previously embraced them: all electronic, hip hop sounds and angular patterns, with Arthur Baker's mix-genius at the centre of it. At its core, is a succinctness that blasts its message in little over sixty seconds but lasts throughout the whole album. If its brevity leaves you breathless and wanting more, there is a 4.38 version to be found on the B-side of 'Possession Obsession' while a 6.38 mix of it was included in that single's 12" version and can be found on the 2004 CD reissue. One critic described it as 'Trebly percussion and fancy slap-synth', but effused nonetheless because of the way it segues into...

'Out Of Touch' (Hall, Oates)

Their sixth and final US number one emerges from the crashing end of 'Dance On Your Knees', leaving the two tracks so intertwined that the 'Out Of Touch' video retains the prior song's final 'dance on your knees' declamation as its opening sequence. Just like 'Kiss On Your List', it's a hit song that arrived through serendipity. It was created not for a Hall & Oates record, but from when Oates was playing around with the new synthesizer technology and came up with something he felt had a classic Philly sound. He thought it might make a great song for The Stylistics, who Arthur Baker was working with at the time. But Baker identified it as a strong chart candidate for Daryl and John themselves. John had the chorus – another concerned with the distance that had developed between Nancy and him – and its key line as being 'You're out of touch, I'm out of town', wanting 'town' to be replaced with a rhyme for 'I'm out of my head when you're not around'. But he was persuaded to put 'out of time' in its place – a rewrite giving the song far more poignancy when Daryl got to sing it. It really is a heartbreaker of a song, switching between faith that things can always be what they were, and the recognition of two people coming apart and needing to stand back and stop fuelling the flames.

It has all the big mid-1980s production elements, but also a feeling of space in its stop-start arrangement, allowing Hall his vocal asides – 'Take a look around' and 'Too much' – while John's backing vocal chants of 'time' as part of the harmonies on the chorus adds to the bittersweet lyrics, and his underpinning of those harmonies into the coda gives Daryl the improvisational space to pick out words to turn almost into a rap, with an admonishing 'out of touch, out of time' refrain at the end. It's just glorious.

'Method Of Modern Love' (Hall, Janna Allen)

Sparse and staccato, the album's second single is best summed by a contemporary *Big Bam Boom* review by Stephen Holden, which set it in the context of Arthur Baker's previous work with Afrika Bambaataa and the Soul Sonic Force 9 ('sharp-edged synthesizer textures, machine-gun clatter of electronic percussion, electronically altered vocals'), describing how Daryl and John 'carried that sound from the street to the fashion showroom ... the sounds of hip hop become one of several key textural elements in an intricately layered musical fabric'.

'We're doing what we always wanted to do, and more of it', Daryl contended in an interview with Roy Trakin for *Creem* during the filming of the 'Out Of Touch' video. 'This record is more upfront. It's got soul, energy. We're playing around with our own history and what's going on around us'. In the same feature, John explained how they'd 'delineated what it is we do. Because we have a lot of people listening to us, it's our duty to stretch ourselves musically, and take our audience along'.

Fair enough, though this one hasn't the timelessness that some of their other songs of the period have assumed. It's a little bit art rock, a little bit rap; a spell-a-long that leaves the listener working out what it is they are spelling. Although it's simple stuff, the spelling leaves out 'modern', and for a moment just sounds like a jumble of letters. Odd.

The vocals are smooth, with Daryl almost as crooner. But otherwise, its wide-ranging and echoing style just feels at odds with Hall & Oates, like they'd stretched themselves a bit too far in trying to be flash and up-to-the-minute.

'Bank On Your Love' (Hall, Oates, Sara Allen)

Even allowing for this being the 1980s, 'Bank On Your Love' is an overproduced bombast, despite having a sense of space and separation with slow booming drum patterns, cowbells, staccato guitar chords, and grandiose lyrics with regal and gambling metaphors liberally sprinkled around. Quite the jumble, in fact.

ZZ Top's Billy Gibbons just about squeezes himself and a tasty lead guitar lick, into an equally cluttered version on an edition of *Live From Daryl's House*.

'Some Things Are Better Left Unsaid' (Hall)

Taking a line from the almost ten-year-old 'London, Luck & Love' as its title, this is Daryl returning to a favourite theme of the rocky grounds love is often constructed upon. It's a laconic, shimmering blue-eyed-soul/soft-rock crossover, which – though busy in that *Big Bam Boom* fashion and with a messy middle eight built around what's almost a mini drum solo – has a quietly understated sadness and sense of loss that is really appealing. Even so, as the album's third single, it only managed to reach 18 in the US.

'Going Thru The Motions' (Hall, Oates, Janna Allen, Sara Allen)

The weakest track is a spluttering, messy and overlong techno dance number that at a dragged out 5:39 already feels like someone has plonked a 12" re-mix bang smack at the start of the album's second side. And, like Daryl's 'Go Solo', at the very point he and John are stretching their creative legs with their embrace of new recording equipment and methods, this four-way co-write with the Allen sisters seems to foreshadow a drifting apart over the next few years. 'Lately, we're going through the motions'.

'Cold Dark And Yesterday' (Oates)

Dark in its title and delivery (and an intriguing contrast as the 'Out Of Touch' B-side), it's tempting to hear this Oates song as being, like its famous A-side, about the state of his relationship with Nancy Hunter as they headed towards divorce; one song being the creeping paranoia of physical separation, and the other a fatalistic take on a crumbling marriage. Not so, according to John, who described its genesis as coming from a throwaway comment G. E. Smith made while the band were on their first Australian tour, sitting on a beach comparing the antipodean summer with the winter they'd left behind in the States. In the liner notes for a *Big Bam Boom* reissue, John said, 'It's always been one of my favourite songs. I think it's pretty adventurous and pretty cool. I wanted to write a song that sounded like Edwin Starr's 'War', that kind of vibe'.

'All American Girl' (Hall, Oates, Sara Allen)

Into filler territory with this really awkward tune, described as the sound of Spanish Harlem in their survey of the urban New York scene, but with such uncomfortable lyrics, particularly around the sleazy spoken word section. 'She's got a Double Bubble with a bossanova back/She's a real hot pepper and I like it like that'. Some things are, it's true, better left unsaid.

'Possession Obsession' (Hall, Oates, Sara Allen)

Oates sings lead on this song that's partly a reflection of the possession-hungry consumerist society that the decade was quickly becoming notorious for, though the city-travelogue video – which features Oates as a taxi driver with varying passengers – suggests it's much more about *emotional* possession. It's a low-key (one might say damp squib) ending to a record that promised so much; playing out in a lacklustre and uninspired manner.

The following year, they had a big moment ahead of them with their contribution to 'We Are The World' and their Live Aid appearance. But the album does have an end of era feeling around it, even if they were appearing to be riding high off the back of a clear run of four successful LPs.

The Arista Years
Ooh Yeah! (1988)
Personnel:
Daryl Hall: vocals, synthesizer, bass, keyboards, guitar
John Oates: vocals, synthesizer, guitar, Linn 9000 programming
Tom 'T-Bone' Wolk: bass, synthesizer bass, keys, guitar, accordion
Pat Buchanan: lead and rhythm guitar
Tony Beard: drums
Mark Rivera: saxophone
Jimmy Bralower: drum programming, sequencing
Sammy Merendino: drum programming, sequencing, timbales
Jeff Bova: synthesizer programming, sequencing
Sammy Figueroa: percussion
Recorded at The Hit Factory, New York
Producers: Daryl Hall, John Oates, Tom 'T-Bone' Wolk
Release date: 10 June 1988
Label: Arista
Chart Placings: US: 24, UK: 52
Running Time: 49:24

Though *Big Bam Boom* would be H&O's final RCA studio album, and they wouldn't record together for another four years, there was one more record to appear on the label. Captured at New York's Apollo Theatre on 23 May 1985, *Live At The Apollo* – with former Temptations members Eddie Kendricks and David Ruffin – contained a mixture of Temptations classics and more recent Hall & Oates material. The two duos met again that July at the US Live Aid concert, while Daryl would also play a two-song solo set that year, with T-Bone Wolk and G. E. Smith at the inaugural Farm Aid benefit show in Illinois.

Kendricks & Ruffin and Hall & Oates seemed to be a match made in heaven; a nostalgia-driven tribute to the roots of Daryl and John's music and a chance for them to pay homage to those earlier singers by regenerating them for a modern audience. While Kendricks had been a founder Temptations member, Ruffin had joined in January 1964: initially as a backing singer, but quickly cementing his place front-of-stage and singing the smash hit 'My Girl'. Other hits followed, but Ruffin was descending into the drug dependency that continued for the rest of his life, breaking with The Temptations for an erratic solo career, later reuniting with Kendricks when he too eventually split with the band. They both re-joined for an unhappy and costly reunion tour in 1982, with Ruffin dismissed after missing dates due to his cocaine dependency and Kendricks suffering the same fate due to the state of his voice after years as a heavy smoker.

Initially, it seems that Daryl and John's idea for that Apollo Theatre show (a benefit for the United Negro College Fund - rebranded as UNCF in 2008) was to involve the other Temptations founder-members Melvin Franklin and Otis Williams, who were still playing in the band, who turned down the opportunity. Interviewed for the *Los Angeles Times*, Ruffin claimed, 'It worked out better this way'. Kendricks saw it as 'a nice gesture by those good ol' white boys. They could have easily done the show without us. We needed them more than they needed us. They've done stuff for us that black folks couldn't do, because they've got the power. It was good of them to remember us. You get used to selfish people in this business. It's a surprise when something unselfish happens'.

The year before, Hall was quoted saying he 'loved The Temptations when I was growing up. They were a major influence on my style. I would have loved to be in the group. If they would have let a young white kid join, I would have done it'.

Recalling the Apollo gig – the Harlem theatre's reopening night – Oates described it in a way that sounded almost karmic: 'We'd been there to see The Temptations just after we first met, and it had been an incredible night. We thought we'd bring things full circle by inviting Eddie Kendricks and David Ruffin on stage with us. I don't know when we had a better show'. But he also saw it as closing off a period in his life: 'I think we didn't know how to top that. I needed to reboot and cleanse my soul'.

Before that cleansing could take place, there was Live Aid to play – again with the former Temptations, providing one of the day's standout moments. They opened with a raucous and strident 'Maneater' before bringing out Kendricks for 'Get Ready', shining the rest of their spotlight on further Temptations classics with Ruffin appearing for 'Ain't Too Proud To Beg' and 'My Girl'. It was a generous moment on the biggest platform popular music had ever experienced. But it also signalled an ending, for the moment at least. And that rehabilitation of Kendricks and Ruffin? However fabulous it was to see them on that large stage, it didn't prevent Ruffin from continuing his drug consumption (to Hall's outspoken frustration), in 1987 receiving a two-year probationary sentence for cocaine use. He died of an overdose of crack cocaine on 1 June 1991. Kendricks succumbed to lung cancer the following year.

Following Live Aid, Daryl and John largely went their separate ways for the next few years. They'd played a couple of dates in May '86 – notably a multi-band benefit show at the Louisiana Superdome in New Orleans, with Huey Lewis and the News – but essentially, the duo was on hiatus.

The previous October, Daryl started work on his second solo album with trusty lieutenants G. E. Smith and T-Bone Wolk. Dave Stewart of synth-pop duo Eurythmics, co-produced with Hall and Wolk – going for a far more accessible sound than the progressively challenging *Sacred Songs*, even if the result was a little pompous and self-important in places. Its release the following August as *Three Hearts In The Happy Ending Machine*, was accompanied by stories of the disbanding of Hall & Oates. Daryl proclaimed: 'This album is very different from what I've been doing in the recent past with John. I think I've undergone a bit of a personality change in trying to lose this standoffishness that I seem to have been dragging around with me for years. The songs came from putting away one era of my life and moving into another. I really like working with John, he's my best friend, but I want to keep things separate for now'.

For John, the changes were more accentuated again as he and Nancy separated. And with Tommy Mottola's ever-present management security blanket also lost as he moved on to become president of CBS, John found himself cut adrift to carve out his own place in the music business.

It was a fairly low-key start, and he wouldn't follow Daryl in releasing a solo album until 2002. Instead, John travelled to Australia and worked with Iva Davies of Icehouse – the collaboration yielding the global hit 'Electric Blue' – then producing the *Small Victories* album for Toronto band Parachute Club.

In a radio interview, Iva Davies recalled hooking up with John as being 'one of the most random stories' that went right back to 1982 and the Icehouse album *Primitive Man*.

I was sitting in Adelaide airport, and this fellow came over – moustache and curly black hair – and he had a cassette of *Primitive Man*. 'Hi, I'm John Oates of Hall & Oates. Just bought your album and loving it'. He just walked off into the airport and I was gobsmacked. Go forward to 1986 and I was on tour in America, and I was in the same hotel in New York for three weeks. Tiny bar, the phone rang, barman picked it up, 'Call for you', and on the end, this voice: 'Hello, it's John Oates, we met years ago... I've got to write songs with you'. I'm not good in that celebrity situation, so I made every excuse not to, but there was no getting out of it, and in due course, he came out to Australia and we spent a week at my house, and by the end, we had a fair slab of songs.

Davies felt 'Electric Blue' was unfinished at that point, but Oates demanded that Icehouse record it and put it out as single, with the judicious promise – or threat – that if they didn't, Hall & Oates would, and it would be a hit: 'And he was absolutely right'.

Oates recalled that in working with Parachute Club, 'They were very innovative, very cool. For me, it was the chance to try something new. I'd been wrapped up in Hall and Oates, and to work with those guys was great. I got to spend a lot of time in Toronto and hang out, so that was fun. They broke up right after that album, so I hope it wasn't me!'.

Daryl and John regrouped in 1988 to record *Ooh Yeah!*, strangely dismissed in Oates' memoir as being an unfocused album that 'my head and my heart were not into'. Considering it's a record with some fairly strong moments and an absolutely top-drawer Oates solo credit in 'Keep On Pushin' Love', it's a strange summing-up, but that's all he has to say about it in his book. At the time, though, he contended:

The magic resurfaced again. That's the reason we are working together: a chemistry that seems to endure. We could have come back together and our songwriting ideas could have been in opposite directions: 'It's not going to work, see you later'. But as it happened, the ideas were very much in synch and it fell together very comfortably and very easily. Daryl and I were both more aware of what our individual contributions to Hall & Oates were, having done separate projects.

According to John, they'd signed a deal to move to Arista Records even before their RCA contract was completed, though Daryl's second solo LP, *Three Hearts in the Happy Ending Machine* also appeared on RCA, and that notion of a new contract being signed before leaving RCA doesn't seem to square with their hiatus. But Arista didn't bring the same level of success they'd previously enjoyed, and they parted company with the label after only two albums.

The new album wasn't going to sound the same as those 1980s RCA albums. Though T-Bone was still involved, the Hall & Oates band had also largely gone their separate ways, so *Ooh Yeah!* reverted back to their 1970s method of gathering session musicians, requiring the duo to – as Oates put it – generate all of the musical energy themselves.

Daryl Hall told the *NME*:

We work together because the world forces us to, but besides that, we know each other very well. We grew up together in an era and region that was musically unique. He's the only person I've met who understood it as well as I did. Having lived through all those experiences together, our relationship triggers a creative spark. You have to step away from your life and continually reassess things. It's okay to base an edge between you which continually spurs the other on. There's a balance along that edge. We get the best out of each other without exploding.

'Downtown Life' (Hall, Oates, Rick Iantosca, Sara Allen)

Opening the album and its accompanying shows, is this genuine stone-cold classic: far better than anything on Big Bam Boom ('Out Of Touch' aside). It's full of funky rhythms, has a muscular middle eight and catchy chorus harmonies where Daryl's vocal asides are totally in synch with what's happening around him, and possesses a strong moral backbone as well. It's New York in all its glory, with the focus on the vibrancy of city life after the sun goes down. For a band so associated with the Philadelphia sound, it's a reminder that New York has an equal influence on Hall and Oates. 'Our roots are in Philadelphia, but our music came from New York', said Oates.

Like a state of the city survey, they focus in, laser accurate, on the changing face of the daytime where stockbrokers have moved in, gentrified the downtown area, characterised as 'Yuppies in black doing white collar crime', who've 'Scared away the local color'. They still can't steal the night, though. Come sun-up, the dawn patrol who'd 'better leave me alone' could be police sweeping the streets for the remnants of the night's activities, or perhaps the early shift of local radio with their overtly cheery starts to the day.

Elsewhere in the lyric, we see Lou Reed, thinly disguised as Velvet Lou, in the days before he moved out to New Jersey. *New Yorker* magazine explained: 'Hall lived in a two-bedroom apartment on Sheridan Square. He'd see Lou Reed walking his dog, and went to clubs like the Mercer Arts Centre and CBGB. 'We loved the music, we'd hang out backstage, but we were never part of it''.

The song's co-writer Rick Iantosca was a music producer who at the time was working with Daryl and John's Temptations friends David Ruffin and Eddie Kendricks. Rumour has it that 'Downtown Life' was originally written for the movie *Beverly Hills Cops II*, but withdrawn for Hall & Oates to use instead. Look out also for the 1989 'Downtown Life (Remix)' 12': particularly the restrained, understated and vocally focused 'Baccapella' version.

'Everything Your Heart Desires' (Hall)
The album's first single and the duo's last US top ten single sounds like a *Voices* reject – Daryl Hall by numbers; a pleasant but totally inconsequential ditty sung to a restless partner who sees the grass as always greener on the other side, or maybe a dominant personality whose mind is closed to his partner's longings and aspirations. Reviewing the album, *The Washington Post* heard it as mid-tempo soul that was reflective of Daryl and John's still recent link-up with Ruffin and Kendricks, noting that the Motown sound had been updated to include second rhythm patterns via the use of drum machines.

As with 'Downtown Life', there's a 12" EP of remixes – '54th Street Extended', '7th Avenue Remix', 'If You Want The World Mix', 'No Words Can Help Dub Mix' – if you really need more of this stereotypical AOR fodder. But you probably don't.

'I'm In Pieces' (Hall, Janna Allen)
Chronologically, this song of unspoken desire – a strong candidate for a single, with its Hollywood soundtrack saxophone intro and expressive Hall lead vocal – was Janna Allen's last H&O co-write, though she also sang backing vocals here on 'Rockability'. Aged only 36, Janna died of leukaemia on 25 August 1993. Hall said, 'I don't think people realise how close we were and how much she influenced me. She was a very interesting person and a very interesting songwriter. Janna was a firecracker. She egged me on'. There's a lovely, poignant moment on one of Daryl's solo acoustic performances on *Live From Daryl's House*, where he dedicates his song 'Somebody Like You' to Janna 'Wherever she is', and glancing over his shoulder... 'Right there, probably'.

Janna's legacy as the final part of the four musketeers alongside Daryl, John and Sara, is a swathe of well-known and much-loved H&O songs: 'Kiss On My List', 'Private Eyes', 'Method Of Modern Love' – a strong core that have her input absolutely central to them. As for 'I'm In Pieces', *The Washington Post* positioned it as the album's 'best song of all; a heartbroken hook so singable, and a performance so perfect, it could pass as a Smokey Robinson composition sung by the original Temptations'. I'd imagine Daryl Hall would take that review any day of the week.

'Missed Opportunity' (Hall, Oates, Sara Allen)

A wistful and regretful ode to things that might've been, with a tangible air of loss and melancholy and an accompanying video showing Hall in an empty but lived-in flat, is a little gem, and at the same time, very much a routine H&O number. It doesn't stand out, yet it's a poignant delight when it surfaces in the running order. With nice harmonies and a good atmosphere, it does very well for itself without breaking new ground or being distinctive.

'Talking All Night' (Hall, Oates)

Being both tongue-in-cheek but still being appealingly sensual nonetheless is a neat trick, and with a jaunty and funky bass line playing against the slow burn of a late-night saxophone, 'Talking All Night' never takes itself too seriously as it runs through the early morning hours, three-quarter hour by three-quarter hour, of two people totally into each other. Here's a little curio, the improvisor, actor and writer Glo Tavarez, self-confessed Hall & Oates superfan, picked this song to talk about on the *Repeater* podcast in 2018, saying how she discovered the duo via 'Maneater' and Spotify. 'I picked this song because it's fun. 'Talking All Night' is like the song of the summer, it's always summer when you listen to it. And he's like 'it's three o'clock, talking all night...' and then he's like 'six in the morning? Time to get up!' It's kind of campy and weird, and so fun'.

'The duo's 'Talking All Night' uses the old convention of counting off the hours of a romantic evening more effectively than anyone in years,' said that *Washington Post* review, before declaring 'the trio of Hall, Oates and T-Bone Wolk, is one of the best production teams in pop today. The three integrate synths and drum machines without ever sounding mechanical and they vary their dance rhythms without ever losing the beat or growing monotonous. Mindless summer pop doesn't come any better than this.'

'Rockability' (Hall, Oates, Sara Allen)

Oates, being interviewed prior to *Big Bam Boom*, is recalled as having suggested one of the tracks would be a number called 'Rockability' and would pose the question: do you have it? It appears, though, that only the title is recycled for this rather cheesy dance piece that might have been a half-decent club number if pushed in the right way, but hardly suggests that they were spoiled for choice in cuts for this record.

'Rocket To God' (Hall)

On first listen, this is a forgettable and slight piece, but it bears repeated listens so its ethereal jazz sounds – led by an impassioned but restrained Hall vocal and a smooth saxophone – coalesce into what one reviewer described as being about 'romantic ecstasy'. Hall said to the *NME*: 'It's a very romantic album, a late-night album, one that reflects everything that's good and positive about personal relationships. Throughout the recording process, I would go home late at night and be so zonked, I wouldn't even read. [I'd] listen to Barry White go round and round in this dream consciousness. I think some of that sensuousness is captured'.

'Soul Love' (Hall, Holly Knight)
Though it wasn't unheard of to see co-writers outside of the Daryl, John and Allen sisters stable credited, 'Soul Love' looks towards future albums in seeing professional songwriters come in on the composing and lyric-writing for H&O records, suggesting, as the next album, *Change Of Season* would confirm, there was an emerging trend towards looking outside of the immediate 'family' for songwriting support. This one, with Pat Benatar, Tina Turner, and Heart contributor Holly Knight, is part of what's been described as the 'love' trilogy that sees out the album. It's just lazy sequencing, to be honest, and it's another fairly inconsequential tune, while 'gimme that gimme that nasty touch' isn't the most romantic of requests.

'Realove' (Hall, Oates)
The most notable thing about this song is a guest appearance from Japanese multi-instrumentalist Keisuke Kuwata of the 1970s band Southern All Stars. It's a curious album addition in that it brings in session players – guitarists Jimmy Ripp and Paul Presco, and saxophonist Lenny Pickett – and seems to have been written as a promotional vehicle for Kuwata. More muscular than the songs surrounding it, it's an interesting new direction and plays out into a delightful shimmer with kalimba-like chimes that could almost segue into the album's final track.

'Keep On Pushin' Love' (Oates)
A sex worker on the tout for business, a metal fan in leathers trying to ingratiate himself backstage, and a preacher man with his hand out for the worshippers' cash, all make for a disparate mix of characters in this John Oates opus. It's the seedy downside of 'Downtown Life', complete with the business guys who give the homeless 'the walk on by' and are almost certainly those yuppies in black we were previously introduced to. The two songs are a perfect pairing as the best opening and closing combo since 'It's A Laugh' and 'August Day'. Sparse synthesizer parts allow Oates to draw his protagonists in accurate detail, while the song builds up to its central message: for everyone to just 'Let your love lite shine'. If that sounds pat, then the sincerity of John's delivery of the verses, coupled with Daryl's vocal embellishments for the chorus and coda, lift it well beyond any of idea of just being cod, heart-on-sleeve, preaching. Inspired in part by the Curtis Mayfield song, 'Keep On Pushing', and having

some of the same musical freeness and core sentiments, and suggesting an answer to the question as to just what Mayfield was wanting to keep pushing, it's gorgeous.

Visiting an *Ooh Yeah!* recording session, *Spin* writer Timothy White tracked the development of the song, which he described as 'a lean, atmospheric slice of rock 'n' soul verve', where *Rolling Stone* found Oates copping 'a sly, Lou Reed-like delivery'. White followed the song from its origins: 'a lot of specific but spacy guitar from Oates ... brisk picking offset by blended rhythm', to the point where, satisfied with the guitar placement, John adds his 'casual bopping vocal ... the pre-rap pacing of some bygone Muhammad Ali haiku'. John's improvisations lead Tom Wolk to work on the arrangement, while John works through his lyric, and 'By the time Hall layers falsetto filigrees into the experiment, Daryl's trading fire with Oates' guitar'. They work through the track over the next few weeks, adding Mark Rivera's saxophone as an understated floating counter-melody, interacting in a way that White viewed – in contrast to the tricky relationships of duos like Sam and Dave or Simon & Garfunkel – as being 'trust, based on shared self-reliance ... Creative contact has probably kept their tensile bond from becoming a booby trap'.

Related Tracks
'Love Train' (Kenny Gamble, Leon Huff)
Released on Sire Records in 1989, Daryl and John revisited their Philadelphia roots with this modernised, and truth be told, a little insipid, cover of the Gamble-and-Huff-penned O'Jays classic, recorded for the soundtrack of the Geena Davis, Jim Carrey and Jeff Goldblum-fronted sci-fi spoof *Earth Girls Are Easy*.

The Gamble and Huff partnership was really taking off by the time Hall & Oates signed to Atlantic. This 1972 hit is an essential part of the Gamble and Huff canon – covered by everyone from The Three Degrees to The Rolling Stones: confirming, as one commentator put it, that the sound of Philadelphia was, of course, for 'people all over the world'. As for this very decent cover, well, you can't top perfection, I'm afraid.

Change Of Season (1990)

Personnel:
Daryl Hall: lead and background vocals, piano and synth, guitars, mandolin, mandola, tambourine
John Oates: lead and background vocals, guitars, bongo, clay drums
Tom 'T-Bone' Wolk: guitars, bass, Wurlitzer piano, percussion, background vocals
Bobby Mayo: Hammond B-3 organ, synth, background vocals
Jimmy Rip: guitars
Mike Braun: drums, percussion
Charlie DeChant: saxophone
Jimmy Bralower: Akai MPC-60 drum programming
Mike Klvana: synth programming
Pete Moshay: sequencing, electronic programming, tambourine
Arif Mardin: string arrangement and conducting on 'Starting All Over Again' and 'Change Of Season'
Recorded at Cherokee Studios, Hollywood, CA
Producers: Daryl Hall, John Oates, Tom Wolk
Release date: 3 November 1990
Label: Arista
Chart Placings: US: 60, UK: 44
Running Time: 56:42

If *Ooh Yeah!* was intended to be a comeback album, its reception and sales gently informed the duo that – though they'd only been apart a few years – time had moved on and their early-1980s stadium-filling run was behind them. Giving the new album *Change Of Season* much more space in his book of the same name, Oates suggests they'd crossed the line between being contemporary stars and veteran musicians. That feels right because it's a journeyman album in the best sense of the word: made by craftsmen, but arguably minus the spark of youthful ambition.

T-Bone and Charlie DeChant were still around, but the Allen sisters were absent. Mottola was away with his new career. The sense of family that had always infused the Hall & Oates setup was fading away – represented by scattergun production credits, and a cast of co-writers, session musicians and backing vocalists (including Siobhan Fahey and Marcella Detriot of Shakespears Sister). It feels, therefore, like a Hall & Oates album for the sake of one, or a contractual obligation – though John described the result as being a soundtrack to where he was in his life at the time.

They settled into a more acoustic feel, ringing the changes in how they sounded and how they looked when John finally shaved off that legendary moustache, a surprisingly symbolic moment. Daryl thought their return to a more acoustic presentation 'makes the song come out, that's what's really nice about it, you really hear what the song's all about'. It equalised them again, in a way that had been lost in the *Private Eyes/H2O* era: two guys sat front-of-stage on stools, feeling easy in their own skins, playing through their tunes. This gave them an appealing road-weary vibe that visually described how they'd aged and matured. 'I think we've grown up a lot', said John, 'I think we've taken a lot more responsibility for our music and ourselves'.

If their 1980s work was informed with their urban environment, that was another change being reflected. Hall had moved to Upstate New York, while John moved to Connecticut and then Colorado, enjoying the outdoor life of cycling and skiing. Hall told *OOR*'s Martin Aston: 'Throughout the '80s, urban dance music moved us, the world, when we lived in New York, but we're just not part of it because we don't live there anymore. Right now, it doesn't feel natural for us to make that music. I think the scene backed itself into a corner. It hasn't played itself out, but it's been overdone and just needs to settle into its proper place'.

But it felt like a closure. Their spell with Arista was an unhappy and truncated experience, Hall bemoaning label-meddling, particularly around the album's lead single 'So Close': which, according to Daryl, Arista boss Clive Davis demanded they re-record for the single, with Danny Kortchmar and Jon Bon Jovi. Hall told *Ultimate Classic Rock*: 'I had this beautiful arrangement, which is on the record, and he made me go in and cut some ridiculous version with Jon Bon Jovi, and I hated it. That's the ultimate version of interference. I was quite unhappy about that'. You'd wonder how the Daryl Hall at the peak of the RCA years would've handled that, but it was a signal that *Change Of Season* could be the last Hall & Oates album. But it wasn't – they re-emerged later in the 1990s with *Marigold Sky*, and they wouldn't be on hiatus again in quite the same way, coming together to play live less regularly and extensively than before, but still keeping the brand alive on the road. But it was an extended recording break that came out of the disappointments of their Arista contract.

In the same interview, John said, '*Change Of Season* was two guys who'd been working together for a long time and were embarking on their own separate ways. That set the tone for everything we've done from that point ... two individuals who enjoy working together, but don't see themselves as joined at the hip'. You could say that, as veterans, they were on the point of becoming a nostalgia act, playing the hits to an appreciative audience. But there were a handful of good recordings left in them yet.

'So Close' (Hall, George Green, Danny Kortchmar, Jon Bon Jovi)
'So Close – Unplugged' (Hall, George Green)
Possibly the most muddled track in the Hall & Oates canon, 'So Close' comes in multiple variants – meddled with by Jon Bon Jovi and Danny Kortchmar, played as an acoustic number in what Daryl thought was its correct form, and rethought again in different ways for the album, the single and the video.

George Green (John Mellencamp's principal writing partner) got a writing credit with Daryl on the 'unplugged' version that closes the album. According to Hall, Green's contribution was as a starting point that Daryl could then run with, with Green coming up with the opening verse and the 'So close, yet so far away' refrain. It's certainly not hard to hear what Daryl would have found appealing about this idea, another of those wistful glances into the past and to those 'what might have been' lyrics that Hall had been playing with as far back as 'Abandoned Luncheonette'. The unplugged version is by far the superior cut: its sparse instrumentation perfectly complementing the ache and regret in Daryl's vocal. Set against it, the full band reimagining feels like a hangover from the 80s, losing the sense and sentiment of the acoustic original, perhaps with the label trying to recoup its investment by turning the clock back to 1983 and completely missing what they had in this song.

'Starting All Over Again' (Philip Mitchell)
Originally released in 1972 on the legendary Stax Records by cousins and duo Mel & Tim (Melvin Hardin and Timothy McPherson) and written by the R&B singer, songwriter, and record producer 'Prince' Philip Mitchell, there's a genuine honesty and touching sense of heart about this very authentic cover version. In his memoir, John all but confirms that part of the reason for choosing to do this one was in resonance with where he and Daryl were at this point, discarding the successes and the image that they'd cultivated in the 1980s and starting, indeed, all over again with something different. It's our duo making homage to the sort of records they'd always loved, a soul standard, captured for a new audience. Paul Pearson, for *Treblezine*, and with emphatic insight, comments that 'to re-establish who they are in relation to each other, they rely on the kind of music that brought them together in the first place.' So true.

'Sometimes A Mind Changes' (Hall)
A warmly familiar Motown, '(Sittin' On) The Dock Of The Bay', feel to the bassline on this one underscores this gentle rumination on growing apart and feels just right following on from 'Starting All Over Again'. For all his vocal dexterities and going off-piste in delivery, Daryl Hall is absolutely at his best with this sort of nostalgia-tinged soul. The sentiment harks back to 'Abandoned Luncheonette' and cherished dreams that escape realisation in the routine of day-to-day life. 'There's a certain poignancy to this song', he confessed. 'It has a lot to do with people around me who I've watched stuff happen to; that problem when you wait too long for something to happen, and then it never happens. That's a big problem in everybody's life, I guess. That *woulda shoulda* kind of thing'.

'Change Of Season' (Oates, Bobby Mayo)
When asked why he virtually used the album title for his autobiography, John said that it was, 'because that title seemed to really exemplify what the book is about. It's about changing, and it's about evolving and trying to change over the years ... the process of maturing. I wrote that song [at] a time when I

was going through a lot of personal stuff – business things, getting divorced, financial things – and I really wanted to start over again. I wanted to recreate my life in a much better way that could take me forward into the future'.

It's a charming and simple tune filled with an inspiring ease – led by Bobby Mayo's quiet but steady keyboards building slowly to a crescendo with his Hammond Organ swirl. It's another song that describes their debt to those Philly soul bands; to Motown and to Stax. And, as it plays out, it's really a joyous ode to the pop single in general.

'I Ain't Gonna Take It This Time' (Hall)
A 3 am in the morning – when the inner voice has nothing useful to say – monologue of anger, frustration, bitterness and sheer desperation to move on from a toxic relationship. It continues the album's theme of personal change, though steps outside of its general air of Philly soul, delivering instead a big power ballad where Daryl can really let loose and give the lyrics a good belting. It could have been a very decent single, but it does shift the mood of the album rather.

'Everywhere I Look' (Hall)
A 'no fault' breakup tune, accentuated with a weepy T-Bone guitar lick, further embellishing the already thickly-layered lyric. But it sounds better on the tour's audience recordings – stripped down to its acoustic foundation and shorn of its overproduction.

'Give It Up (Old Habits)' (Terry Britten, Graham Lyle, Hall (Additional lyrics))
Recorded as 'Old Habits Die Hard' by the Neville Brothers in 1987, and then again the following year by Crystal Gayle, H&O here reconstruct the song: shifting the lyric sentiment and providing a much bigger production than that of the original's quirky sprightliness, while Charlie DeChant's saxophone really marks it out as reimagining rather than a cover. There's a suggestion that it came from more label-meddling: Clive Davis having been keen to include it. Like 'Starting All Over Again', it does fit the album's retro vibe. It almost comes across as a distinct song: not better than the original, but – melody aside – just different.

'Don't Hold Back Your Love' (Richard Page, Gerald O'Brien, David Tyson)
Released as the album's second single, this is quite possibly yet another example of the label interference Hall has bemoaned in regard to their Arista contract, given that they took the unusual step of releasing someone else's song as a single. And while Daryl puts his heart into a minor classic like the Mel and Tim cover, here he seems to be phoning it in and going through the

motions. The website *Coffee For Two* succinctly sums it up, saying it 'sounds exactly like mid-'80s detritus spruced up for the dawn of the '90s', and believing that the duo 'had to know they were working with material that was dismal compared to the pop wonders that fuelled their heyday'. Harsh, but in truth, despite some really good material appearing on this record, tracks such as this one display the slippery slope that they'd found themselves on since leaving RCA and taking that initial hiatus at the peak of their powers.

'Halfway There' (Hall)

Forgettable, uninspired, and described in a contemporary review as having a 'modicum of soul in its yearning', this track never really gets going, despite having over five minutes to do so. It's a typical Hall lyric of a relationship that doesn't want to let go but doesn't have a clearly foreseeable future either. The arrangement shares that sense of uncertainty, frittering away on repeated phrases that feel more like an attempt to flesh out the demo than a fully-rounded H&O song.

'Only Love' (Oates, Jo Cang)

Written by John with Joe (credited as Jo) Cang – a London-born singer-songwriter whose debut album *Navigator* was released on Arista the year after *Change Of Season*. Joe told me the following:

John's a very down-to-earth guy, not starry. When I was signed to Arista, at the time, the MD was a guy called Roger Watson – a friend of John's, a social friend, they were mates really. So I think that's how (Daryl and John) came to know about me. John got in touch to say 'Would you be up for a link-up?'. I said I was going to be in America to see my brother in New York, and he came out with this great phrase: 'How do you feel about light aircraft?'. I'm a Londoner, man. I don't know anything about light aircraft. I have no feelings about them. 'Oh, because I fly, I'm a pilot, and I fly to all my gigs, and I might be flying in...'. Anyway, the weather was bad, so we weren't doing that. He was living in Connecticut at the time – an amazing place – so we drove up for the weekend. He had his studio in his house, as one does, very nice, and we got on well. We wrote two songs really fast, from scratch, just sitting in the room, all quite natural. He (said) 'Yes, great, I'll get an engineer over to record it'. We started on 'Only Love', and all the power went off. Now, I was a dope smoker. He's not, he's very healthy. So there's a barbecue while the power's off, and I'm getting a little bit inebriated, and then the powers back on and it's 'Let's go' ... So we recorded them both, did the demos, quite simple, late in the night and into the next day. So it was a weekend really, and 'Only Love' went straight on the album. I thought they did a really good version of it. 'War Of Words' turned up later, and I think he worked with someone else on that as well. I seem to remember there's a different publishing split; maybe another writer took a little bit of it: that's fine.

'Heavy Rain' (David A. Stewart)

Martin Aston, for OOR, considered 'Heavy Rain', written by Daryl's *Three Hearts In The Happing Ending Machine* co-conspirator Dave Stewart, as being clearly the most classic H&O-like track. 'We know each other really well,' said Daryl, 'and I think he tried to write a song like us. It really fitted in – he wrote it about him and Annie [Lennox] and it worked so well because we've shared all this duo stuff.'

A gentle, thoughtful start with female backing vocals (including Stewart's then-wife Siobhan Fahey) smooths the way for Hall's entrance into a song that feels like it reflects the distance that had opened up between the duo – even when you know it's not written about them – before it breaks into an urgent Stewart lead guitar. With guest bass from Bob Glaub, and production by Hall and Stewart, it feels like a track cut outside of the main sessions: perhaps sans Oates completely.

Related Tracks
'Can't Help Falling In Love' (George Weiss, Hugo Peretti, Luigi Creatore)

The duo's take on this Elvis Presley classic appeared on a 1990 *NME*-released double album of Elvis covers *The Last Temptation Of Elvis*, an eclectic gathering of artists as diverse as The Reggae Philharmonic Orchestra, Fuzzbox, Vivian Stanshall and Bruce Springsteen. And while the standout cut is arguably The Jesus And Mary Chain's swaggeringly sleazy rendition of 'Guitar Man', 'Can't Help Falling In Love' certainly made the jangle-pop generation sit up and take notice of a duo that existed well outside the indie-cool comfort zone. John told this author: 'Daryl and I, in addition to being songwriters, we have a great respect for other songwriters, and that respect translates into our ability to interpret. You want to interpret something so that you're comfortable with it and you've made your mark on it. But always, in the back of your mind, honouring the original is very important. We both have a reverence for other songwriters and songwriting in general'.

On his *Mississippi Mile* delta-blues solo album, Oates returned to Presley for reinterpretation: 'It's a very delicate balance to treat a classic song in a way where you honour the original but at the same time try and make it your own. I think the key to [*Mississippi Mile*] was the song 'All Shook Up'. I really had not intended to make an album, and I was sitting in my home studio, playing the guitar and this sort of bluesy, delta-blues style riff and for some reason, I began to sing 'All Shook Up' over it, imposing the original melody and words over this minor-key delta-blues thing. I loved it. Elvis was an icon and an inspiration to me. I thought he was just the coolest thing that ever walked the face of the Earth [laughs]. I had to define what a song is; a song is lyrics and melody. I think the chord changes are up for grabs, the arrangement is up for grabs, the approach, the attitude, the energy. They don't constitute the song; the song is the lyrics and the melody. I kept those things pretty much intact and it was the approach, the chord changes, the feel and the groove that I messed with'.

'Philadelphia Freedom' (Elton John, Bernie Taupin)

John and Taupin wrote this as a tribute to tennis legend Billie Jean King and her Philadelphia Freedoms team. H&O recorded it for the 1991 John/Taupin tribute album *Two Rooms: Celebrating The Songs of Elton John & Bernie Taupin*. Daryl and John are in good company with the likes of Sinead O'Connor, The Who, Tina Turner and other top-drawer performers, though the highest plaudits on this compilation are reserved for Kate Bush's enduring cover of 'Rocket Man'.

The Reunion Years
Marigold Sky (1997)
Personnel:
Daryl Hall: lead and background vocals, keyboard and percussion programming, guitar
John Oates: lead and background vocals, acoustic guitar
Tom 'T-Bone' Wolk: guitar, bass
Dave Bellochio: keyboard and percussion programming, acoustic guitar
Ken Sebesky, Paul Pesco, Dave Stewart: guitar
Shawn Pelton: drums
Peter Moshay: percussion
Charlie DeChant: saxophone
Recorded at A-Pawling Studios, Pawling, New York; Marion Recording Studios, Fairview, New Jersey
Producers: Daryl Hall, John Oates, Dave Bellochio
Release date: 17 September 1997
Label: Push Records
Chart Placings: US: 95, UK: 179
Running Time: 57:40

With the 1990s moving relentlessly onward, and no sign of any new material, their fans could've been forgiven for thinking the two Arista albums signalled closure for the duo. Daryl had again embarked on solo work, releasing his third LP *Soul Alone,* in 1993. Though the album title referenced the music that formed the backbone of his life, and notwithstanding the song title 'I'm In A Philly Mood', *Soul Alone* leaned more towards a light pop-jazz groove. While T-Bone and Charlie stepped across from the Hall & Oates band, it was another ensemble session-player recording, with Sara Allen credited on a couple of songs and Janna's final song for Daryl 'Written In Stone' closing the record. She passed away only two weeks after the album's release.

Soul Alone and its singles did little business, and the follow-up – 1996's *Can't Stop Dreaming* – appeared in Japan only, with a wait until 2003 for its US release. Hall said in a 1993 interview: 'I had the idea of doing a solo album, that was the concept'. And it's as bland a record as that nothing statement sounds – written in the studio, on the fly, when he'd traditionally prepared ideas and snippets before coming into work. He then relied on Sara, and on the Average White Band's Alan Gorrie, to help him assign those tunes some lyrics afterwards. He spoke of the process as though it was a positive outpouring of fresh ideas, borrowing some stylings from London's acid jazz movement: 'Brand New Heavies, those sort of people, and I think I was subtly influenced by those kind of chords, which are slightly different to those I'd normally use. I let it enter my body, and I threw it out in another way'. But they must have been salutary experiences, a lesson that, try as he might, and though he'd slowly, over the years, seemingly become the first among equals in Hall & Oates, as a solo artist, sales and recognition were that bit harder to come by.

John, on the other hand, was taking to his newfound freedom with a growing sense of ease about himself, enjoying his outdoor sporting interests rather than feeling the need to continue as a musician first and foremost. Through his love of skiing, he met Aimee Pommier in Aspen, and in 1994 she became Aimee Oates; their son Tanner arrived two years later. John still played those occasional Hall & Oates shows – 'Just to keep the cashflow going' – but there were no new equivalents to Icehouse or Parachute Club to keep his hand in the world of writing and production. Effectively, he'd retreated to a simpler but satisfying life.

The duo regrouped again for 1997's *Marigold Sky*, though it's commonly believed they'd worked on material as a follow-up to *Change Of Season* as early as 1992, only to have Arista pass on it. Arista also rejected *Marigold Sky*, causing the duo to take a stake in the newly-formed Push Records, with Push also releasing Hall's *Can't Stop Dreaming* album: much delayed in the US.

Marigold Sky was one of those late-period H&O records that seemed to be a Hall solo record in all but artist name, with Oates credited on vocals, mainly backing ones as it transpired, and a couple of acoustic guitar contributions. It's another album he overlooks in his memoir, suggesting that while he was happy with the irregular live performances, his interest in new studio work was diminishing. As the new century unfolded, Oates would discover the sweet spot of his own style and voice, producing some great work, though it would first take a misfire solo record to get there.

But with *Marigold Sky*, it seemed the writing was not just on the wall, it was right there in Brad Hitz's front cover shot, taken in the Bahamas at Hall's Harbour Island home – the pair walking barefoot and casual on the white sands, into the sunset: suggesting this to be a farewell album in all but name. Reflecting in hindsight on those years between *Change Of Season* and *Marigold Sky*, Daryl conceded, 'I was on my own. I was living out of the United States and I wasn't seeing John much. I have to tell ya, we came together, almost reluctantly, to do *Marigold Sky*. We were flexing our muscles as individuals'. He explained in a BBC radio interview at the time of the album's release:

We spent so much time travelling around, working and writing and recording and doing everything, that I think we lost a bit of objectivity about what it was that we do. In order to continue, one needs to stop occasionally, or at least once in life. So, we did what we did, and I'm glad it happened. In any relationship, whether it's the kind of relationship John and I have, or with Sara Allen, I think we have a freshness in our lives because we weren't together constantly. We've never been in it for the money you know, that's truthfully – money's good, we love money, but it's really about the fun of making music and the need to make music, and that's what's always sustained us and stimulated us. That never goes away.

'Romeo Is Bleeding' (Hall, Alan Gorrie)

Reflecting on H&O's departure from Atlantic Records after the weirdness of *War Babies*, remember how John claimed that the label had dropped them in favour of Scottish funk/R&B crossover act Average White Band, though it's generally considered the move to RCA was by choice and engineered by Tommy Mottola? Curiously, the two groups gravitated towards each other in the 1990s, with various AWB members playing in the Hall & Oates band, and Daryl striking up a friendship with founder AWB member and bassist – and writer of their memorable UK hit 'Let's Go 'Round Again' – Alan Gorrie. Appearing as a backing vocalist on Daryl's 1993 *Soul Alone* album and as bassist on the opening track, Gorrie also received a co-writer credit on the minor Hall solo classic 'I'm In A Philly Mood'. When AWB cut their 1996 album, *Soul Tattoo*, Daryl appeared as a guest vocalist on 'I Wanna Be Loved', and by the time of *Marigold Sky*, Gorrie had seemingly become Hall's go-to lyric collaborator, having also worked on Hall's *Can't Stop Dreaming* LP. That Daryl would seek out different writers to work with wasn't anything new, think back to Warren Pash on 'Private Eyes', who Hall had cultivated for some time as a potential partner, and who was aware of Daryl also exploring options with other songwriters. 'These days we've have more of a family of writers that we work with', Hall explained to the BBC in 1998, 'it's the exception rather than the rule that [John and I] will write a song together'.

A *Washington Post* review noted the pair tilting 'its self-described 'rock 'n' soul' formula in the rock direction', with the emphasis on electric guitars and muscular dance beats. Particular praise was reserved for 'that moment in the chorus when an ear-grabbing melody locks into a hip-grabbing rhythm ... especially in the synth-rocker 'Romeo Is Bleeding'', though the reviewer also named 'Throw The Roses Away' and 'Marigold Sky' as highlights. Another heard this opener as 'a peppy number that could easily have found its way onto one of the duo's mid-'80s albums'.

In its sleek groove and big production values, 'Romeo Is Bleeding' is as close to classic Hall & Oates as anything from their latter-day albums... if only Oates had a greater presence. A standout track, it sets the tone of a breakup album, invoking that great lover of yore Casanova, along with Shakespeare's tragic Romeo, who died for love – the song coming only a few years before Daryl Hall and Sara Allen's longtime relationship would reach to its own end.

'Marigold Sky' (Hall, Oates)

Second track and things are cracking on nicely, more big production values and full-on pop sound, and more break-up laments to a long-term situation edging to its conclusion. 'Was I ever yours?/Were you ever mine?' Daryl asks, reflecting on just how long a broken heart can take to heal. 'Marigold Sky' is rich, evocative and totally involving as you live the heartfelt pain it articulates. And what you're already taking from these songs is time moving on, a sense of ageing and the aching feel of melancholy that's to come. 'The idea of love is complicated', said Daryl, 'so I think a good love song has to be complicated. To just write a song, 'I love you, I can't live without you', that's sort of stating the obvious'.

'The Sky Is Falling' (Hall, Sara Allen, Alan Gorrie)
More heartbreak, and the sense of having someone leave your life with no chance of reconciliation. As it goes along, it becomes clear that they front-loaded the album with the best material, and what would've been side two (if released on vinyl) sees them revisit their own 1970s tone. That's not to say the record's earlier material isn't in the Hall & Oates vein though: 'The Sky Is Falling' could've come from somewhere around the *Voices* era. Hall claimed, 'We've invented a certain kind of music that's identifiable; certain kinds of melodies, harmonies, song structure; certain lyrical point of view. It's hard to describe, but when you do these things, it sounds like Hall & Oates'.

'Out Of The Blue' (Hall)
This could almost be a sequel to 'The Sky Is Falling' – an old lover calling up 'out of the blue' and igniting angst in the narrator who believed that love was 'water under the bridge, long gone', leading him to lament that his number hadn't just been thrown away. If it sounds familiar, it's because (at least to these ears) it's a pretty direct rewrite of 'Bank On Your Love' from *Big Bam Boom*.

'Want To' (Hall, T-Bone Wolk, Alan Gorrie, Sara Allen)
If you were looking for a *third* Hall & Oates member, you might consider Tommy 'Gino The Manager' Mottola, or find a case for it being Sara Allen. But in the end, you'd have to say bassist Tom 'T-Bone' Wolk (here receiving a rare writing credit), who arguably provided the Hall & Oates band with something similar to what Steve Van Zandt represented in the E-Street Band: the glue that holds the arrangements together.

Nicknamed T-Bone by H&O guitarist G. E. Smith (in honour of blues guitarist T-Bone Walker), Wolk also played with the likes of Elvis Costello, Carly Simon and Billy Joel. After first appearing on *H2O*, Wolk pretty much became Hall and Oates's indispensable right-hand man, their musical director, referred to by Hall as 'The ampersand in Hall & Oates', and on another occasion as 'My musical brother ... one of the most sensitive and good human beings that I have ever known'. For Wolk, being part of Daryl and John's story was as comfortable as putting on a glove, though he was happy to consider himself more modestly as 'That guy with the hat'. When a heart attack suddenly took him in February 2010, he was working on Daryl's solo album *Laughing Down Crying*, and was about to appear with Hall & Oates on *Late Night With Jimmy Fallon*.

'Any instrument he touched resonated with a sensitivity and a skill level that I have never experienced while playing with any other musician', said John. 'He possessed an encyclopaedic knowledge of styles and musical history, which he referenced to support all the artists he played with over the years. He made everyone he played with better'. Another time, John confirmed, 'We made it a joke all the time, but it wasn't a joke: he was the ampersand in Hall & Oates. It was true. Even before he passed away, when I was playing something, in the back of my mind, I would say, 'How would T-Bone do it?'. He's the yardstick'.

Asked about his bass-playing in the studio, Wolk referenced Paul McCartney and how, circa 'Paperback Writer', the Beatle had come to the conclusion that the bass part was best left to be recorded last. Wolk said, 'That was a significant turn in production for me. I like to come in later, and all my parts come from the singer and/or the melody. I pay attention to the flow of it all, and I do my best to just support that'. What a support indeed.

'Love Out Loud' (Hall, Sara Allen, Alan Gorrie)
A sort of blues/country barroom rocker with horns giving a sleazy backdrop. It sounds like a Keith Richards solo number, circa Keef's *Main Offender* album, sharing a vibe with that record's '999'. It's slight, but tasty. I'm glad it didn't miss the cut, but truthfully, it belongs somewhere else.

'Throw The Roses Away' (Hall, Alan Gorrie)
An intimate piano ballad with a sentiment of heart-wrenching finality, where love has broken down, and letting go and moving on is the only way to achieve peace of mind, and still, *Marigold Sky* seems the prelude to Daryl and Sara's split. In this deeply-reflective mood piece, it feels for all the world that Daryl is pouring his heart out. With the 'sweet memories', all the dreams, and the plaintive cry of 'I don't know if I'll ever find someone like you again'. They never married, though he'd been married to Bryna Lublin between 1969 and 1972, divorcing around the time Daryl first met Sara. Subsequent to their parting, he married Amanda Aspinall, divorcing four years before her death in 2019. Daryl also had an on/off relationship with actress Marcia Strassman, and a son – Darren – with Andrea Zabloski in 1983. So, all told, the Hall/Allen relationship – they are still friends – is a complex story of emotional twists and turns far beyond the scope of this book. And the truth of their commitment to, and expectations of, each other are probably only understood by the singer of rock and soul, and the lady who, to the outside world, seemed his soul mate.

'I Don't Think So' (Hall, Dave Bellochio, Sara Allen, Alan Gorrie)
A light tune that roots itself in the mid-1970s of *Bigger Than Both Of Us*. It's rather inconsequential, but it's delightful to hear John's backing vocals invoke 'The good times and the bad times' simply because it creates a warmly-nostalgic aura that takes the listener right back to those early RCA albums.

'Promise Ain't Enough' (Hall, Oates, Porter Howell, Dwayne O'Brien)

Principally an Oates song, co-written with Howell and O'Brien from the Nashville country band Little Texas, who were on hiatus at the time, though Hall chipped in on lyrics. This first of a string of *Marigold Sky* singles reached six on the US Adult Contemporary charts. It's an easygoing love song and a proper counterpoint to those surrounding it, that might reflect the point John had reached in his life. He talked of how he was 'thinking about getting married when I came up with the idea for the song'. That suggests that the idea had been around for a couple of years, since John married Aimee Pommier on 28 November 1994, but it perfectly encapsulates a feeling of waiting for that right person.

In interviews for *Marigold Sky*, John referred to the solo albums he'd made during their hiatus, mentioning family, childbirth, homemaking and how, post-Nancy, he found the right way to be settled and content: 'We decided – mostly it was (Aimee's) idea – that the only way we could make it work in the crazy lifestyle I lead, is to be together all the time and share it as a team. We brought up our son that way. He went on the road when he was five weeks old'.

Reacting to reviews that suggested 'Promise Ain't Enough' was a return to 1970s Hall & Oates, Daryl noted, 'That's exactly why it was chosen as the first single. We wanted to get to the Adult Contemporary market because we thought it was probably our core market, and we thought that song would work on the AC format. We're thinking about other songs for other markets'.

'Time Won't Pass Me By' (Hall, Oates, Dave Bellochio)

A companion piece to 'Promise Ain't Enough'. If most of what came before is Daryl's story, here's John again celebrating finding fulfilment, with nights that are no longer lonely, and how he's been 'lucky on the second try'. It's a mellow, chilled-out glossy piece that could've been a 'silver' album outtake. And it's lovely to hear Daryl and John's vocal interplay as if from days gone by. Dammit, we miss that, they were so good at it.

'Hold On To Yourself' (Hall, Dave Bellochio, Alan Gorrie)

Charlie DeChant's trademark intro saxophone sound, roots this song (a cautionary admonishment to nurture and nourish your inner self) in the H&O pantheon. But the sax is mixed lower in the rest of the track than he deserves, and there's a bigger production trying to bust out of this understated number. But it's filler, and evidence that the album's lengthy 57 minutes cry out for the selection discipline of vinyl – not uncommon for CDs, though this was the first Hall & Oates album to not appear on vinyl.

'War Of Words' (Oates, Jo Cang)

I asked Joe Cang about the increasing amount of Hall & Oates co-writers.

It's kind of understandable. I don't know them well enough. I met John's family, his son; they're really down to earth people. But any duo that's been in the public eye, there's always rumours, and you're going to have some disagreements; but bands are just weird, the marriage analogy. There's no right and wrong in art, it's all subjective. I remember him saying to me, 'I write with Daryl, and it's like putting your old shoes on – it's comfortable, but they're your old shoes, and sometimes they don't go with your outfit and you want to mix them up'. It was an honour to work with them.

Another introspective acoustic mood piece, John really comes into his own in the second half. It's another heartfelt reflection, and though it sat in the drawer for so many years since that weekend of writing with Cang in Connecticut, it really earned its place on a Hall & Oates album.

Do It For Love (2003)

Personnel:
Daryl Hall: vocals, keyboards, electric guitar, string arrangement
John Oates: vocals, guitar ('Love In A Dangerous Time')
Tom T-Bone Wolk: bass, acoustic/electric guitar
Mickey Curry: drums
Jeff Catania: electric/acoustic guitar
Todd Rundgren: electric guitar, lead and backing vocals ('Someday We'll Know')
Greg Fitzgerald: acoustic/electric guitar, programming and sequencing, backing vocals, keyboards
Billy Mann: acoustic guitar
Paul Pesco: acoustic guitar ('Forever For You', 'Heartbreak Time')
Shep Goodman: programming and sequencing, keyboards, strings, acoustic/electric guitar, bass
David Sancious: keyboards
Kenny Gioia: programming and sequencing, keyboards, strings, drums, percussion
Additional Musicians: Mike Shimshack, Greg Bieck, Peter Moshay, Mark Taylor, Jack Daly, Steve Wolf, Steve Torch, Audrey Martells
Recorded at A-Pawling Studios, Pawling, New York; Protopia-NYC; Rive Droite Music, UK; Stella Studios, UK
Producers: Daryl Hall, Brian Rawling, Sheppard Goodman, Kenny Gioia, Mark Taylor
Release date: 11 February 2003
Label: U-Watch
Chart Placings: US: 77, UK: 37
Running Time: 56:16

One glance at the credits for this final (to date) Daryl Hall & John Oates album of new material tells you it's another Daryl Hall and friends record, rather than a proper Daryl and John LP. Here, Oates appears on guitar and lead vocal only for his song 'Love In A Dangerous Time' (which had recently appeared on his first solo offering *Phunk Shui*). He also sings as part of a three-way lead vocal with Daryl and Todd Rundgren on 'Someday We'll Know'. Elsewhere, Oates is on backing vocals only. Given the multiple recording locations (including two in England, where early, but aborted, work on the album started in 2001), you'd wonder how involved he was in the process. Those initial England sessions seemed to be a search for collaborators, as though they needed outside influence and direction to get the creative juices flowing, though if that's truly the case and their own heritage and legacy wasn't enough to draw on, as it absolutely should have been, why bother? With John largely anonymous for much of the record, it became another hodgepodge of producers, longtime associates and session players. It's not a bad record at all but doesn't sit easily in the catalogue.

The duo were burned by their experience with Arista Records, while Push released very little material and seemingly left *Marigold Sky* in a rights quagmire that made it the other exclusion from the comprehensive *Do What You Want, Be What You Are* career retrospective (for very different reasons than the deliberate ignoring of *Beauty On A Back Street*). So the duo struck a deal with music packagers Doyle-Kos Entertainment, to create their own label: U-Watch. Daryl told *Billboard*: 'John and I like to work independently. We are at our best when we are not soldiers in an army. We baulk and we walk away from any situation where we are not in control'. Talking about *Do It For Love* as being just that: a labour of love, he complained how 'It started with us trying to please the corporate world. Then we walked away from that and said, 'We're just going to make this record the way it's supposed to be made'.' The album did at least revitalise their radio presence and got them talked about again. Daryl described the record as being the start of something, as though it was getting the ball rolling for a new Hall & Oates era, but it simply wasn't.

'Man On A Mission' (Hall, Oates, Paul Barry, Steve Torch)

Daryl Hall is definitely the 'Man On A Mission' in question here, and in keeping with much of what's to come, he dominates proceedings, with John Oates relegated to backing vocals. But hey, it's a dynamic album-opener, full of hooks, sing-along lines, and a great tune, an overlooked latter-day classic for the duo - that clear proviso aside – and with a very simple and direct lyric. He's on a mission to get the girl, and he can't let that idea go, and that's it, basically. But despite the thinness of the idea, at 3:44, you're left wanting more. 'The mission is to get outside the box', suggested Daryl of the album. 'It's a very homemade kind of record. It's a culmination of all the different stylistic directions we've gone in, pulling it all together and focusing it. It's a very organic record; it's emotional; great songs and melodies'.

'Do It For Love' (Hall, Oates, Billy Mann, Paul Presco)

Alongside VH1's *Behind The Music* Hall & Oates segment came the compilation *VH1 Behind The Music: The Daryl Hall and John Oates* Collection. Largely another unimaginative roll call of the usual suspects, it did end with a tantalising glimpse of new material that would find its way onto *Do It For Love* – 'Heartbreak Time', the title track, and a recording of Daryl's solo song 'Someone Like You', radically retitled as 'Somebody Like You'.

'Someday We'll Know' (Gregg Alexander)

Long-time, though occasional, collaborator Todd Rundgren turns up here for a cover of New Radicals' 'Someday We'll Know'. New Radicals likely narrowly missed a hit with this second single from their 1999 album *Maybe You've Been Brainwashed* – the band dissolving prior to its release, with its writer Gregg Alexander moving into production and as a songwriting gun-for-hire.

The song's tale of loss, evoking the pilot Amelia Earhart, the Titanic, and Atlantis amongst its metaphors results in a moving and shared vocal performance from Hall, Oates and Rundgren – John's opening to the song is a particularly strong moment - while Todd also plays a sympathetic lead guitar line that weaves its way through the song's outro in a quite reflective manner. One of the very best covers in the Hall & Oates canon.

'Forever For You' (Paul Barry, Mark Taylor, Steve Torch, Oates)

Totally uninspiring and instantly forgettable, 'Forever For You' is adult-contemporary balladeering at its blandest. The critic responsible for an *Uncut* hatchet-job review might well have had this song playing when describing the album as teetering 'near the pretty vacancy of today's blue-eyed chart acts', though to be fair, the quick-fire review also acknowledges 'the duo's ear for a hook' and 'Hall's still-soaring voice'.

On that thorny subject of the term 'blue-eyed soul', Hall, interviewed in 2011, had come to a view that made him feel uncomfortable about its application. 'American music has always been this thing of interplay between African and European influences. The way it goes back and forth on both sides is where the vitality is. People like the Righteous Brothers – they were singing real soul music. They didn't know what label to put on it and put – what I thought – was a racist term. You don't call someone a brown-eyed opera singer if they are a diva in opera and happen to be black'.

'Life's Too Short' (Hall, Oates, Billy Mann)

This is a warm, acoustic and thoroughly catchy deep cut that should be more widely known. Exuding feelings of regret, loss and an ache to rekindle a love that the narrator's 'crazy spell' seems to have torn up in a moment of madness, it gets under the skin with a keen sense of purpose.

'Getaway Car' (Gary Haase, Billy Mann)

Country singer Susan Ashton's raw and bare original version of this Springsteen-esque song on her 1999 album *Closer* is better than this overly smooth version that sacrifices sentiment by becoming (excuse the pun) a middle-of-the-road, adult-contemporary take. John is still missing in action, guitars provided by co-writer Billy Mann and the ever-dependable T-Bone. The lead and backing vocals are all Daryl. *Do It For Love,* by the way, avoids the ignominy of *Marigold Sky's* non-mention in John's autobiography by the skin of its proverbial teeth, mentioned in a one-sentence acknowledgement during his co-author Chris Epting's afterword.

'Make You Stay' (Hall, Billy Mann, Greg Fitzgerald, Tom Nichols)

The outside writing teams that make up much of *Do It For Love*'s writing credits never really get a handle on whether they're producing material for an MOR soft-rock outfit or some sort of boy band. So they lean towards the latter while keeping in mind the former. What they're absolutely not doing is writing for Hall & Oates. It's like someone got them together in a room, put on a side of *Beauty On A Back Street*, let them have a quick listen, and sent them away to write some stuff based on what they could remember. It's dire, instantly forgettable and pointless.

'Miss DJ' (Hall, Billy Mann, Greg Fitzgerald, Tom Nichols)

One commentator described this as 'positively modern in its light space-funk, reminding me that Pharrell [Williams], as great as he can be, has nothing on Hall & Oates'. Inexplicably popular amongst most contemporary reviewers, this track is an unusual mix of spacey and disjointed: as if it's two separate songs at the same time and the listener's job is to somehow separate them. Despite that, it still manages to be thin and lukewarm.

'(She) Got Me Bad' (Greg Fitzgerald, Tom Nichols)

It's getting very telling now – Hall & Oates revealed as a well that's creatively running dry. Concurrent with *Do It For Love*, Fitzgerald and Nichols wrote a couple of songs on Kylie Minogue's 2001 album *Fever*.

This fairly fairly generic middle of the road affair that doesn't stretch Hall's vocal dexterities, which are often overridden and found sulking in the background while the 'backing vocals', featuring Greg Fitzgerald alongside Daryl and John (for what reason, the long-time fan might, quite fairly, wonder) dominate. Doesn't that relegation out of the central focus and side-lined from the spotlight take the point of Daryl Hall away?

'Breath Of Your Life' (Hall, Greg Fitzgerald, Tom Nichols)

By now, it's clear this is another split-side record (despite being CD-only). But rather than the commercial side and experimental side of yore, or the adult-contemporary A-side and nostalgic B-side of *Marigold Sky*, *Do It For Love* has a good side, and a side that descends into forgettable blandness. It perks up near the end, but it's getting there that's the challenge. It's exactly as the *Past Prime* website put it: 'If Hall & Oates re-present themselves as a boy band in 2003, they are a boy band for the retirees or for the wine drinking that comes after the book club has finished their serious matters'.

I defy anyone to play this track multiple times and remember how it goes two minutes later. It's *that* transient. The chorus is a kind of Michael Jackson pastiche, but this really isn't Daryl Hall & John Oates. It just isn't.

'Intuition' (Paul Barry, Billy Mann, Mark Taylor)

Another one minus John, and both men are missing from the writing. No wonder it's a pale imitation of a Hall & Oates album. 'Intuition' is a paint-by-numbers soft-focus ballad, and it's hard to believe it's even Daryl singing. By this point, my own intuition is that there really wasn't enough Daryl and John material to properly warrant this album.

'Heartbreak Time' (Oates, Paul Barry, Mark Taylor, David Bellochio)

This starts like it could be an *Abandoned Luncheonette* outtake! But then, it arrived via the VH1 compilation rather than as part of the album sessions. Like its immediate predecessors here, it's another late-night smoothie. But it seems to have an authenticity that 'Intuition' and 'Breath Of Your Life' lacked. Now, if you were played it and told it was a 1970s number that missed the cut, you'd think it a very nice outtake without believing it should have got on an album, but that's still better than what's surrounding it.

'Something About You' (Hall, Sara Allen, David Bellochio)

This is possibly a *Marigold Sky* leftover, given the writing credits for that album's co-producer and Sara Allen (by now separated from Daryl). It's a pleasant, likeable soft-focus ballad that – while rather slight – shines above many of the other tracks.

Sara and Daryl have remained friends, with Sara contributing to *Behind The Music* and making a brief appearance on an edition of *Live From Daryl's House*. In recent years, her focus has been on the Buddy System charity, which works to provide autistic children with assistance dogs.

'Love In A Dangerous Time' (Oates, Arthur Baker, Tom Farragher)

Originally coming from 1991, and initially being John's thoughts on the AIDs epidemic, this song was recorded for his *Phunk Shui* solo album and is reimagined again here: 'When I resurrected the song for (*Phunk Shui*), it was timely and pertinent to the things going on in the world today.'

John told interviewer Michael Cavacini: 'It was about a changing world as I saw it; AIDS, violence, turmoil. I prefer my solo version, because the music is more ominous and less pop'. It's a more minimalist rendition, with John's vocal possessing a greater intimacy and the music being sparser, drawing the listener in, in a confiding and thoughtful manner, and as the roots element of his music has grown ever more prevalent in his solo records since, there's probably an even more stripped back version to be played. But its appearance here is fortunate, since, sitting at the end of the last Hall & Oates album of principally new material, it sees out what's honestly a lesser work in the catalogue with a late burst of quality.

The Covers Albums
Our Kind Of Soul (2004)

Personnel:
Daryl Hall: lead and background vocals, keyboards, acoustic guitar, string arrangements and conducting
John Oates: lead and background vocals, electric guitar
Tom 'T-Bone' Wolk: guitars, bass
Greg Bieck: keyboards, drum programming, sequencing
Charles DeChant: saxophone
Additional Personnel:
David Sancious: backing vocals, keyboards
Bobby Eli, Jeff Catania: electric guitar
Steve Jordan: drums
Lenny Pickett: horns
Robert Shaw, Cenovia Cummins, Carol Pool: violin
Stephanie Cummins, Sarah Hewitt-Roth: cello
David Spinozza: string arrangements and conductor
Recorded at A-Pawling Studios, Pawling New York; Great Divide Studios, Aspen, Colorado; The Clubhouse, Los Angeles, CA
Producers: Daryl Hall, John Oates, Greg Bieck
Release date: 26 October 2004
Label: U-Watch
Chart Placings: US: 69, UK: 86
Running Time: 69:28

After 2003's *Do It For Love*, Daryl and John released two more albums – *Our Kind Of Soul* in 2004, (the title perhaps reflecting Len Barry's 1967 album *My Kind Of Soul*), and for the 2006 holiday season, their long-mooted Christmas album *Home For Christmas*. The former was mostly a covers album (with three new songs) surveying the soul scene from the 1960s to the 1980s, and the latter Christmas album was mostly standards but included John's 'No Child Should Ever Cry On Christmas', and the Daryl/Tom Wolk/Greg Bieck song 'Home For Christmas'.

Daryl enthusiastically pronounced *Our Kind of Soul* to be 'the real essence of what I am about musically. Through these songs, the listener can hear the core of what I am as a soul singer. It's my real deal'. Long-term fans might be forgiven for thinking this was plainly obvious and that this, and the Christmas record, simply confirmed what *Do It For Love* had indicated: that the H&O partnership had finally run out of steam. Still, covers albums have been a card to play since as far back as Bowie's *Pin Ups*, and this was, as John said, 'a cool collection of classical music' – which he must've felt to be as much of a vindication of the music of his youth as he'd joyously reflected all those years ago on 'Back Together Again'.

Reflecting on *Home For Christmas* (originally a Trans World Entertainment release, but later made more widely available), John considered it as 'actually one of my more recent favourites; a brilliant album and the last we did with T-Bone. T-Bone had a lot to do with that album, and it's just a great, great record'. As neither of these albums are key studio albums in the Hall & Oates catalogue, I'll touch on both briefly here but without the deep dive their main canon receives in this book.

'Let Love Take Control' (Hall, Oates, Billy Mann)
Despite being predominantly a covers record, it starts with a likeable original song that lyrically is almost a manifesto for the record – urging the listener to 'Hold onto that sweet, sweet soul'. It's a richly-arranged piece, with some nice harmonies and a thick soft-rock sound.

'Standing In The Shadows Of Love' (Lamont Dozier, Eddie Holland Jr., Brian Holland)
The Four Tops' follow-up to their standard 'Reach Out I'll Be There' takes us right back to 1966 and a classic Motown tune from the Holland/Dozier/Holland stable.

'I'll Be Around' (Thom Bell, Phil Hurtt)
This was originally the B-side of The Spinners' single 'How Could I Let You Go'; reaching the top of the US charts and staying there for five weeks. British record buyers knew them as The Detroit Spinners, to avoid confusion with the UK folk group of the same name.

'Used To Be My Girl' (Kenny Gamble, Leon Huff)
No H&O soul covers album could be complete without a Gamble and Huff tune, and this O'Jays number is a stone-cold classic. On the website *Ultimate Classic Rock,* Daryl described The O'Jays' appearance on *Live From Daryl's House* as 'one of my favourites. I've grown up with them creatively and grown up with them physically, from the Philadelphia connection. I went straight to the church of soul with (O'Jays vocalist) Eddie Levert'.

'Soul Violins' (Hall, Greg Bieck)
This heartwarming tale of a lost lover unexpectedly returning was largely written in Daryl's Bahamas home immediately preceding the album sessions: 'I draw from real life, and that song came alive, and I knew it would be right for the album'. It's rather gorgeous, and its notion of those 'sweet soul violins' being so right, playing in tribute to ease something, is very affecting.

'I Can Dream About You' (Dan Hartman)
Dan Hartman apparently wrote this song with Hall & Oates in mind. But according to Daryl, he offered it to them just after they'd finished an album

(possibly *H2O* given the timing). Undeterred, Hartman had it placed in the film *Streets Of Fire*, scoring him a hit when it was released as a single in 1984.

'Don't Turn Your Back On Me' (Hall)
Daryl said he wrote this verse while on tour for *Do It For Love*, and it was something he'd sing as part of the improvised vocal coda to 'Forever For You'. The audience reaction encouraged him to make something more out of it. A mellow acoustic number with a harder-edged lyric undertone, it's another latter-day H&O song that works delightfully.

'Fading Away' (Warren Moore, Smokey Robinson, Robert Rogers)
This was originally the B-side of The Temptations' 'Get Ready', released in 1966 and written by Smokey Robinson. Check out Smokey's appearance on an edition of *Live From Daryl's House* where he takes the lead on 'Sara Smile'.

'Neither One Of Us' (Jim Weatherly)
The full song title was 'Neither One Of Us (Wants To Be The First To Say Goodbye)'- in 1972, Gladys Knight & The Pips' final Motown single before they moved to Buddah Records. In its original form, it was a country song, recorded by its writer Jim Weatherly.

'After The Dance' (Marvin Gaye, Leon Ware)
Marvin Gaye famously wrote this about a woman he spotted in the audience of the TV show *Soul Train*. In sales terms, this 1976 slow-burn ballad was a lesser entry in Gaye's canon but became a blueprint for his later work.

'Rock Steady' (Aretha Franklin)
Aretha Franklin is another artist who it would seem unimaginable to leave out, considering the crossover with the musicians Daryl and John played with on their early Atlantic LPs and her presence on the label herself. 'Rock Steady' was a 1971 single from her Atlantic album *Young, Gifted And Black*, with Arif Mardin among its producers and including *Abandoned Luncheonette* drummer Bernard Purdie. It almost feels like Daryl and John coming full circle.

'Love TKO' (Gip Noble, Cecil Womack, Linda Womack)
This was written for soul singer David Oliver and originally appeared on his 1980 *Here's To You* album. The better-known version (from the same year) is by Teddy Pendergrass – triggering Cecil and his wife Linda (soon to evolve into Womack and Womack) to become (as Cecil Womack's obituary in *The Guardian* put it) 'an in-demand songwriting duo'; their output described as 'emotionally draining adult love songs, sweetened by infectious Philly beats'. Co-writer Gip Noble revealed that the boxing term TKO here represented being beaten up by love: 'I had just left a relationship when I wrote it, so I could relate to the idea'.

'What You See Is What You Get' (Anthony Hester)
This was a hit on Stax Records for Detroit band The Dramatics; its title a catchphrase by African/American comedian Flip Wilson. The original is an appealing, brassy, Latin-tinged tune. The H&O version is an authentic steamy, slow-moving, nighttime rendition that keeps to the original vibe.

'Can't Get Enough Of Your Love' (Barry White)
The first single from Barry White's 1974 LP *Can't Get Enough:* released as 'Can't Get Enough Of Your Love, Babe'. Remember how Arista Records liked to steer Hall & Oates towards particular covers, to Daryl's frustration? They also insisted on Taylor Dayne jettisoning her 'I'll Wait' as the first single from her *Soul Dancing* album, in favour of cutting a version of this tune.

'You Are Everything' (Thom Bell, Linda Creed)
More Philadelphia-soul legacy material with this 1971 hit for The Stylistics, co-written by their producer Thom Bell. Daryl said of the early Philly scene of which The Stylistics were a part: 'I started with those people; they were my friends. I played with The Stylistics, played keyboards; I was a session musician'.

'I'm Still In Love With You' (Al Green, Al Jackson Jr, Willie Mitchell)
A 1972 single from the album of the same name by Al Green. A *BBC music* website review describes the LP as 'Green developing a suave romantic tone', and it must be said that Daryl Hall is sublime in bringing that out in this rendition.

'Ooh Child' (Stan Vincent)
As with 'I'll Be Around' this is another classic (originally stylised as 'O-o-h Child') that made the leap from B-side to A-side – first on the back of the Chicago-based Five Stairsteps single 'Dear Prudence' before achieving recognition for itself in Philadelphia in summer 1970.

Related Tracks
Other editions of *Our Kind Of Soul* have come with bonus tracks – including a live version of 'Me And Mrs. Jones' (Kenny Gamble, Leon Huff, Cary Gilbert; originally recorded by Billy Paul) and 'Without You' (Tom Evans, Pete Ham; first released by Badfinger on their 1970 *No Dice* album). There are also single edits of 'I'll Be Around' and 'I Can Dream About You' as extras on other editions.

Home For Christmas (2006)

Personnel:
Daryl Hall: lead and background vocals, keyboards, acoustic guitar, string arrangements
John Oates: lead and background vocals, guitars
Tom 'T-Bone' Wolk: guitars, bass
Greg Bieck: programming and keyboards
Charles DeChant: saxophone
Additional Personnel:
Michael Payne: guitars
David Sancious: organ, piano, backing vocals
Shawn Pelton, Matthew Payne: drums
Klyde Jones: backing vocals
The London Session Orchestra: strings
Gavyn Wright: concertmaster and first violinist
Isobel Griffins: conductor
Vic Frasier: librarian
Recorded at Studio Five Grand, Harbour Island, Bahamas; Sarm West Studios, London; A-Pawling Studios, Pawling, New York; Great Divide Studios, Aspen, Colorado; Abbey Road, London
Producers: Daryl Hall, T-Bone Wolk, Greg Bieck
Release date 3 October 2006
Label: U-Watch
Chart Placings: US: -, UK: -
Running Time: 50:07

'Overture/The First Noel' (Rob Mathes, Trad.)
Your author, a Cornishman, learned something when writing up this opening track. It's that 'The First Noel', known in its earliest form as 'The First Nowell', derives from Cornish origin! Setting the tone for these traditional folk melodies, which are given a fresh, well-thought-out makeover, it's rather nice, though Daryl's vocal improvisations do stretch it a little.

'It Came Upon A Midnight Clear' (Edmund Hamilton Sears, Richard Storrs Willis)
From the old country to the new – this derives from an 1849 poem by Edmund Sears (then serving as a preacher in Wayland, Massachusetts), set to music by Richard Storrs Willis. Rather than relating biblical stories as most carols do, it's thought to be Sears' rumination on the Mexican-American War, which had recently ended.

'No Child Should Ever Cry On Christmas' (Oates)
If you can't pile on the syrupy sentiments and horrendously-cliched lyrics when

you're writing a Christmas song, when *can* you? 'Toys and laughter/Yeah that's the way/It's supposed to be'. John didn't miss his chance.

'Everyday Will Be Like A Holiday' (William Bell, Booker T. Jones)
Originally a 1967 Christmas hit for William Bell – co-written by Booker T. Jones of Booker T & The M.G.'s – this could've made the cut for *Our Kind Of Soul*. *Hot Press* declared his version the greatest Christmas record of all time. Like Jona Lewie's 'Stop The Cavalry', it probably wasn't conceived as a Christmas song, but its heart and understated sentiment are perfect as such.

'Home For Christmas' (Hall, Greg Bieck, Tom Wolk)
As the album's other original Christmas song, this is much more effective than John's stab at the genre, feeling much more like a warm H&O song where the festive element is incidental.

'Christmas Must Be Tonight' (Robbie Robertson)
This was written (by Robbie Robertson from The Band) from the viewpoint of a shepherd in the Christmas story. Listeners over the years have considered it a lost Christmas classic. Despite later being on the *Scrooged* soundtrack, it's a lesser-known entry in The Band's catalogue, let alone as a Christmas song – and that's a huge shame, as H&O's version demonstrates.

'Children, Go Where I Send Thee' (Trad.)
An African/American gospel song of indeterminate origin, and a smile-inducing choice, Daryl and John having fun with its story celebrating 'the little bitty baby'.

'Mary Had A Baby' (Trad.)
This traditional song of unknown source – cited as being discovered on St Helena Island, South Carolina – was first mentioned in Ruth Crawford Seeger's *American Folk Songs For Children* in 1948.

'The Christmas Song' (Mel Tormé, Robert Wells)
This is more popularly known as 'Chestnuts Roasting On An Open Fire', and is supposedly the most-performed Christmas tune of all.

'Jingle Bell Rock' (Joe Beal, Jim Boothe)
Daryl and John have another stab at this one, twenty years on. They must really like this song!

'O Holy Night' (Trad.)
This carol – originating from an 1843 poem by Frenchman Placide Cappeau – is the perfect ending to a rather nice album. Its mix of standards and lesser-known Christmas songs is a perfect Christmas Day soundtrack.

Postscript

The responses to *Our Kind Of Soul* were muted at best, a three-star *Guardian* review describing it as coming up short compared to the original versions and the duo's own 'golden-era masterpieces'. The reviewer suggested that a little too much reverence for those soul standards had held Daryl and John back from stamping their own identities on proceedings: 'Presumably, they decided that radical interpretation would have been disrespectful, and so plumped for high-class imitation. Masterful harmonists still, Hall & Oates do themselves a disservice by being slaves to the rhythm'. Tough love, but nothing compared to one review that called the duo 'bad taste '80s mullet heroes ... It's easy to accuse them of *plastic* soul, but this collection is nauseatingly safe; the aural equivalent of an airbag'.

There's little sense, though, that after *Do It For Love*, with its multitude of contributing writers, that either Daryl or John had much appetite for creating new Hall & Oates material. They continue to tour what's effectively a greatest hits package, though digging out the occasional audience-pleasing deep cut, such as 'Las Vegas Turnaround' or 'Is It A Star', but overwhelmingly basing their setlist on the giants of their catalogue. That can delight a mainstream audience even while it frustrates the more knowledgeable fans. They operate now in an era where the notion of basing a set around revisiting a particular album has become commonplace, but seem to have no particular interest in going down that road, as John told me when I interviewed him for *R2* magazine:

Artistically, it would be interesting and fun, but I think we'd have to do a very long show: play through the album and then come out and do some of the hits. We have a core set. The hit songs are almost carved in stone, and we like to play those songs. We play them because they still sound good. If a song starts sounding tired and old, we set it aside for a bit and then come back to it. In my solo shows, I like to touch a bit more on the *Abandoned Luncheonette* album: an album that's very important to our career and our lives. We take requests from the audience. Sometimes someone will yell something out and if we can do it, we'll do it. That keeps us on our toes; keeps us interested. But the one thing we'll never do, is to turn into this human jukebox or do – God forbid – a medley of our hits. To me, if a song is not good enough to play in its entirety, why bother? We have a hardcore group of fans who know all the albums and will go out of their way to stump the band. They'll hold up the most obscure titles you can think of, and (laughs) we have to have some selective perception and ignore certain things! But on the other hand, it's fun for us. Someone will hold up a card with some wacky song from 1974, and if we can do it, we'll do it.

That's not to say new material has not been mooted. Around the time the 2020 coronavirus pandemic took hold, it was rumoured the duo were preparing for a new album, and that might yet come to fruition. But generally, they've both been dismissive of the need for fresh work, preferring to see their catalogue as complete.

Interviewed for his 2011 album *Laughing Down Crying*, Daryl was relaxed about the perception of his 1980s records when 'people would snipe at me for the string of songs that have become – for want of a better word – *classics*. I tried to shy away from that sound. But then I just decided to go with it ... We have our body of work, and we're very happy with it. Creatively, I think we want to go in different directions as far as new music'.

They were inducted into the Rock and Roll Hall of Fame in 2014 – an overdue accolade, one might think, but reflective of a new scene. Contemporary artists have sought them out for collaboration (Oates in particular), sampled their work and joined them on tour, though co-headline tours with 1980s contemporaries such as Tears For Fears and Squeeze, have become more the norm. Against a backdrop of black and white photography hailing from the duo's Atlantic days – and to a soundtrack of 'Rich Girl' – John expressed in his understated and dignified way, a belief in the importance of the roots of American music:

That's why we're all here. I want to thank a young couple in New York City in the early 1950s, who bought a '47 Chrysler and decided to move my sister and I to Pennsylvania (Hall: 'About fifteen miles from my house'). I heard big-band music. They took me to an amusement park and I heard Bill Hailey & The Comets in 1953. And if it wasn't for that move to Pennsylvania [*gestures towards Hall*], I wouldn't be here. I was born at the right time. It was a great time to be in Philadelphia. A hotbed of incredible music happening in the '60s. It defines the way I think about music and the way I write songs, the way I play.

Daryl used the same podium to simply lambast the Hall of Fame for the omission of Todd Rundgren, The Stylistics and Chubby Checker.

Hall is not prolific in releasing records. His principal creative interest of late has been the *Live From Daryl's House* webcast, with 82 episodes produced between 2007 and 2016 and further instalments in 2020. He compares it to the studio-bound BBC music show, *Later... With Jools Holland*, where the piano maestro often sits in with the bands. After a lifetime of being on the road, now the musicians and the music come to Daryl Hall, and he's able to play with a multitude of acts – well-known or otherwise – in an intimate setting where muso-chat and even the process of setting up to play becomes part of the broadcast experience. 'It's a very organic, old-school approach to music. It's really just musicians playing, with the minimum of technology. You know, acoustic guitars, basic keyboards, real drums. I end up getting some really interesting guests, who I can interact with in a very creative way'.

John Oates' appearances on *Live From Daryl's House* were limited to the show's early years but were special for that. The three-way acoustic version of 'Had I Known You Better Then' with T-Bone Wolk adding an extra flourish to this song from the early days, was simply a little bit of magic, and there's a great version of 'Possession Obsession' to search YouTube for. But it's a Daryl Hall project, and those rarely crossover with the concept of Daryl Hall & John Oates, though anything from the duo's catalogue is considered fair game for interpretation by the guests. There was a very moving edition (No. 30) in tribute to 'The guy with the hat' – Tom Wolk – with past and present H&O-band luminaries extolling this master musician.

John Oates has released a handful of solo albums, all very different in style to 2002's *Phunk Shui*, and principally exploring his love of delta blues and country. He described his 2011 *Mississippi Mile* album as being, 'from a songwriting standpoint, from a guitar-playing standpoint, singing ... everything that mattered to me as a musician before I met Daryl and we started working together. This was the stuff I was into; this is what turned me onto music and gave me a dream of pursuing a career in music. The artists, the songs, the style – it has a wide range from early folk, folk-blues, to early R&B and rock 'n' roll: it really runs the gamut'. He recognises and values the freedoms the H&O success has given him, and now feels it doesn't matter whether it's in a big stadium with Daryl, or a low-key venue among friends and for an audience that understands he's far more than the overlooked-sidekick stereotype. He makes the most of that freedom.

Believe it or not, it's now one of my more fertile musical periods. This incredible foundation that Daryl and I created together has enabled me to do other things, and I love it. So rather than rest on my laurels, I take advantage of that. A lot of younger artists feel like they took inspiration from what we accomplished, and they reach out to me. I think, in a way, it's interesting because sometimes they reach out thinking it's going to be this nostalgic thing, and yet I come bringing a completely different energy. I've been playing with jam bands and here again playing with lots of great bluegrass musicians, and this is all part of my background, and yet very few people know that. They think I was born with a moustache and playing 'Maneater'! But I had an entire musical life before that.

Reflecting on the Hall & Oates story, John really sums it up:

We had the really good fortune of starting out in a time that tolerated creative experimentation. That environment doesn't exist anymore. Our first three albums were experiments, and each one was different. None of them were commercially successful, but the record company believed in us and allowed us to make these creative mistakes, which allowed us to get to wherever we were going. The albums each had their own personality, and there was a reason for each one of those albums sounding different. Where we recorded... like we'd recorded in L.A. in the middle of the '70s, using studio musicians, and even though we had some success, we said, 'That's not really us', and we developed our own band. The first album we recorded with our own band was *Along The Red Ledge*, so the energy in that album – and it's one of my favourites – came from it being the first opportunity to record with our own band. And that directly led to the success of the '80s when we began to produce ourselves. It was a step-by-step process, and each album is significant in representing something we were trying to do or trying to get to.

Compilations and Live Albums

Without a doubt, you could fill your shelves with Daryl Hall & John Oates compilation albums: they proliferate. And I don't just mean *Past Times Behind* and its subsequent revisions and additions (perhaps get *Fall In Philadelphia* if you want a comprehensive round-up of the 1968-1971 demos) – which we'll ignore here as being off-catalogue – but the regularly-appearing multitude of releases that collect the best-known singles. These continue to appear with regularity while the source material lies, seemingly unloved and uncared for, in record company vaults. Oh, for a proper reissue programme to collect these in properly curated form! So, what follows is certainly not comprehensive but is a pointer to the most significant compilations, along with the notable live albums.

Compilation Albums
No Goodbyes (1977)
The original official Atlantic compilation LP, with the three Arif-Mardin-produced tracks recorded after *War Babies* – only available on this collection – until the 1996 set *The Atlantic Collection* (which included 'It's Uncanny' and 'I Want To Know You For A Long Time') and the career retrospective *Do What You Want, Be What You Are* (which included 'It's Uncanny' and the third track 'Love You Like A Brother'). This is really worth having as representing a moment in time: the early promise of the Mardin sessions and a peek into the progressive rock sidestep of Todd Rundgren's take. It doesn't go for the obvious tracks ('She's Gone' aside), so there's no 'Abandoned Luncheonette' or 'Is It A Star'.

Rock 'N Soul Part 1 (1983)
The biggest and best-known compilation, with the obligatory new single inclusions of 'Adult Education', 'Say It Isn't So', and the live cut of 'Wait For Me' for the hardcore collectors. That it contains only one Atlantic-era track – the 'She's Gone' 7" edit – is simply because this is a *Greatest Hits* LP in all but name. Though some bemoan the exclusion of 'Family Man', it's hard to imagine a better summing-up of the singles, even if the two new songs don't quite hold a candle to the surrounding material. Despite the 1970s songs included, it's so quintessentially a 1980s album, it's sometimes hard to remember it is a compilation, but introductory collections like this, create hardcore fans. Discogs. com lists 112 versions of this album worldwide. The 2006 RCA CD reissue – retitled *The Hits: Rock 'N Soul Part 1*, and declaring on its cover sticker that 'Your Adult Education Starts Right Here' – finally adds 'Family Man' and 'You've Lost That Lovin' Feeling', along with liner notes from T-Bone Wolk.

Do What You Want, Be What You Are (2009)
This most comprehensive, career-defining four-CD compilation takes in the early singles by The Temptones and The Masters, before picking up the pre-Hall & Oates track 'Perkiomen'. It then surveys the whole catalogue, with

the exception of *Beauty On A Back Street* and the contractually unavailable *Marigold Sky*. But it includes five previously unavailable live cuts from their show at the New Victoria Theatre, London on 3 October 1975; a *Change Of Season* outtake called 'Storm Warning' (originally by The Volcanos); a *Private Eyes* outtake titled 'Don't Go Out' (much heavier and more experimental than anything on *Private Eyes*; a Daryl Hall acoustic demo 'Have You Ever Been In Love', and a reworking of a lost 1971 demo called 'Dreamer'.

Live Albums

Livetime (1978)

The first official Hall & Oates live album, recorded on 8 December 1977 at Hersheypark Arena, Hershey, PA. It has its critics – for the sound and often-perceived flat performance and the poor quality vinyl it was pressed on – and has no rarities to get excited about. In his memoir, Oates brushes past it in a couple of sentences, dismissing it as a record company cash-in on the then-trend of live LPs. It's true to say that neither the band nor fans hold this rather slight record in much regard.

Live At The Apollo (With David Ruffin and Eddie Kendricks) (1985)

This is a joyous recording of a standout evening, also released as a VHS video at the time. It's split between a Temptations medley, the Sam and Dave number 'When Something Is Wrong With My Baby', and a set of Hall & Oates songs. It's far from a typical Daryl Hall & John Oates live set, but for its sheer joy and zest for legacy, it's certainly one to own.

Ecstasy On The Edge (2001)

Recorded on 30 October 1979 at Denver's Rainbow Music Hall on the *X-Static* tour. The rarity here is the cover of the Conley/Redding/Cooke song 'Sweet Soul Music': first released by Arthur Conley in 1967. This must be Daryl and John's homage to a homage, given the original was also a celebration of soul – name-checking James Brown and mentioning songs like 'Going To A Go-Go', 'Love Is A Hurtin' Thing', and 'Mustang Sally'. Here it's used for a meet-the-band intro section where each musician, in turn, plays a solo. Elsewhere, the tracks mostly pre-date *X-Static* – culled from better-known singles and *Along The Red Ledge* – but it is an energetic and dynamic set. It emerged as one of a number of off-catalogue US radio show releases: mostly later withdrawn after various label objections.

Live In Dublin (2015)

This live album is the best capture of current-day Hall & Oates, also released as a DVD on the Eagle Vision label. Here's my *Record Collector* write-up under the strapline 'We can go for that':

Hall & Oates brought their Philly-soul to Dublin in 2014: the first time – as Hall frequently reminds the enthusiastic audience – the duo had ever played there. Replete in sunglasses and uttering the obligatory 'man' at the end of most of his repartee, he's the epitome of the ageing but cool rock star; Oates his affable counterpoint. They might not play together so much these days – Hall with his *Live From Daryl's House* web series; Oates recently releasing a series of very good bluegrass records – but despite close-on 45 years together, they still sound unbelievably fresh. They don't try to religiously recreate their songs, instead coming up with interpretations that are honest to their source but contemporary in outlook. 'Out Of Touch' gets a slightly harder edge; I Can't Go For That (No Can Do)' reveals itself a nicely pliable opportunity to kick loose a little while, thankfully, eschewing the rapping that Hall brought to it in the 1980s. The set is centred on the hits, but with room for some classic album tracks as well, delving back to *Abandoned Luncheonette* for 'Las Vegas Turnaround', or turning to *Bigger Than Both Of Us* for the lesser-known single 'Back Together Again'. And, as their Dublin debut, it's clear from this well-shot footage, that both enjoy the occasion.

The Solo Albums
Daryl Hall
Sacred Songs (1980)
Recorded in 1977 with then core Hall & Oates band members Caleb Quaye, Kenny Passarelli, and Roger Pope appearing alongside Daryl and co-conspirator Robert Fripp, *Sacred Songs* was famously shelved by RCA for three years before interest from music journalists, fermented by Fripp, secured it a modestly successful release. At the time, Fripp held the view that 'Had *Sacred Songs* had been released when it was made, it would have put Daryl in category with the Bowies and the Enos' but thought that the delay had lessened its impact. Fripp had an additional vested interest in its release, conceiving it as a trilogy with his production work on *Peter Gabriel II* and his own album, *Exposure*, an idea lost to RCA's reluctance in releasing it. Yet, despite being erratically stodgy and inaccessible in places, it's an intriguing pointer to how Hall's career might have developed had Hall & Oates stopped before reaching their 1980s heyday. While it shares nothing with the H&O of 'Sara Smile' or 'Rich Girl', it does build on the more envelope-pushing sonics of tracks such as 'Falling' in an adventurous, if oft indulgent and ultimately unsuccessful way.

Three Hearts In The Happy Ending Machine (1986)
From the big production and glam rocker riff of its opener, 'Dreamtime', Hall's second solo record positions itself well away from the challenging art-rock of *Sacred Songs*, instead being a stylised and orchestrated take on the excesses of the 1980s, with Daryl positioned grandly at its centre. If anything, it's the sound of a commercially recognised musician being given his head in the way that label bosses just wouldn't fund these days. Perhaps RCA read the writing on the wall for the duo and felt they had to run with the frontman in his new endeavours – and there's a lot to like about the result. But it's very much rooted in its time, often sounding like an overblown Hall & Oates album rather than a distinctive Daryl Hall record, which *Sacred Songs*, for all its accessibility issues, certainly was. 'Dreamtime' gave Daryl his only top ten *Billboard* single and is one of the genuine highlights of his work away from Oates, and his co-write with Dave Stewart and Sara Allen, 'I Wasn't Born Yesterday', is authentic and heartfelt. But there are also some definite Daryl-by-numbers tracks amongst the selection here, unfortunately. Hall, however, claimed this one, and *Sacred Songs*, as being 'the most impactful albums to me', and said how he '[Finds] no fault with either of those albums'.

Soul Alone (1993)
Not so much the change of direction that this album sometimes gets attributed as being, *Soul Alone* is more like Daryl refining a particular element of his work, accentuating the soul and blending it with a contemporary light jazz feel. As such, it feels at ease with itself, as though he's now realised that he's

nothing to prove beyond the bounds of Hall & Oates and can stretch himself a little while glancing backwards to who he once was. 'I'm In A Philly Mood', he croons, and you feel that little sparkle of nostalgia smoothing its way out through his vocal in a delicious confection of hazy dreams and wistful memories. Elsewhere, it works effectively as an album of moods rather than of stand-out tracks, though the regretful 'Stop Loving Me, Stop Loving You' has an ache to it that's as melancholy as any of his Hall & Oates break-up songs, and his delivery of Janna Allen's 'Written In Stone' with its testament to timeless, unconditional love, is pure emotion.

Can't Stop Dreaming (1996)
The lesser-known album in Hall's solo catalogue, partly because of its Japanese-only original release, took until 2003 to make a US appearance. I've touched in the main text of this book how Daryl's throwaway description of its inception as 'I had the idea of doing a solo album, that was the concept' is reflected in the vanilla record that ensued. That said, he does a gentle and contemporary take on 'She's Gone' that gives this evergreen tune a fresh makeover, with a keen sense of being delivered by an older voice that adds new depth to the song's regretful loss. Oates would also occasionally recut H&O classics, with both finding ways to channel their own distinctive styles onto the songs they'd made together. Otherwise, *Can't Stop Dreaming*, as a record to play in the background, is, well, nice... and, to be honest, as bland as that description makes it sound.

Laughing Down Crying (2011)
Hall's first, and to date only, album of the 21st Century found himself rediscovering his mojo on a record that he claimed was 'a very aggressive album. It's got a lot of heart. It deals with a pretty intense emotional landscape'. As he did on *Soul Alone*, he cherry-picked from the textures and styles he'd employed over the years ('the box set of my mind ... elements from the early days all the way through today') and delivered a supple and classy collection where he sounds immaculate. Commercially, it was never going to do the same business as one labelled '... and John Oates', but perhaps the satisfaction of a sophisticated and intimate album had become more important than simple sales units. On its liner notes, he opens by saying that 'you can tell from this collection that I've been through a lot', and that, of course, included losing Tom Wolk to that heart attack early on in the sessions. But it's a return to form, with Hall having a near clean sweep of writing credits and embracing his past with aplomb.

John Oates
Phunk Shui (2002)
Though John would find his own voice as time went by, and largely by returning to his early love of blues and roots, it would take this misfire to set him on the

road to being a solo recording musician, an attempt to extend something of the Hall & Oates sound to his own album and creating an unsatisfying muddle in the process. *Uncut* magazine conceded it was 'mostly efficient self-penned funk-lite and acoustic soul' but wrote off his cover of 'Electric Ladyland' by suggesting that 'Hendrix's psychedelic edges get smoothed into oblivion'. Oates thought the album 'a hodgepodge of styles', and it's clearly an uncertain step into solo recordings that's faded into obscurity; a stepping-stone and no more, really.

1000 Miles Of Life (2008)

A marked improvement over *Phunk Shui*, John recorded his second solo album in Nashville, where he's returned to several times since, and which he considered 'a great city for music ... it doesn't matter really what kind of music it is, it doesn't have to be country music'. It's a quiet, reflective record, one that he conceded had a spiritual element to it; he was thinking about mortality: the people he'd lost in recent years, a heart attack that his father had suffered. 'It's a little down, a little sombre', he told *Souls & Sounds*, 'This album wasn't about writing hits; it was about things that are close to my heart'. A thoughtfully involving album, it signposts the direction his work would take in the future.

Mississippi Mile (2011)

This is the album on which Oates found his post-Hall & Oates voice through an exploration of the music that had ignited his own love of music and started him on his career path. He described it as 'Everything that mattered to me as a musician before I met Daryl and we started working together. This was the stuff I was into; this is what turned me on to music and gave me a dream of pursuing a career in music. The artists, the songs, the style ... it has a wide range: from early folk, folk-blues, to early R&B and rock 'n' roll, it runs the gamut. I wanted to look at the touchstones, the things that were most important to me. There were many other influences, of course, but I had to be realistic and just try and touch on the things that meant the most to me'. He talked about the tunes that had influenced his approach to the record. 'I began to look at these songs which had become my personal repertoire over, and I hate to say it, the last fifty years. If I was with a group of people and we were just jamming or picking, I play these songs. 'Make Me A Pallet On Your Floor' or 'It's All Right' by Curtis Mayfield, or a Chuck Berry song, these are like baby food to me in a way'.

The Bluesville Sessions (2012)

Though John's discographies would typically list this as a live album, it's a valid part of his studio catalogue as well, being a radio station studio run-through of much of *Mississippi Mile*, by the John Oates Band. I had this to say about it for *R2* magazine on its release:

> On the face of it, this 'live in the studio' album replicates much of John Oates's recent Mississippi Mile album, comprising a large portion of that record's

delta-blues covers and John's own songs performed in that style. That's what the tracklist tells us, but there's a lot more to this album. When R2 talked to Oates last year he gave us his notion that 'a song is lyrics and melody. The chord changes are up for grabs, the arrangement is up for grabs, the approach. They don't constitute the song; the song is lyrics and melody'. That's why this record is a valid release even with its debt to Mississippi Mile. In deciding to record in the studio, with no overdubs, the set-list that the John Oates Band had been playing for the previous six months, they've added further vibrancy and passion to the earlier album's arrangements. That idea of reinvention is also evident as the band plays out the set with a Hall and Oates classic, 'Maneater'. It's removed from the original but stands on its own feet, a terrific encapsulation of the way Oates sees the pliability of the songs he plays.

Good Road To Follow (2014)

Originally conceived as a collection of digital singles but converted to an album release as Oates discovered that his audience wasn't of the downloading persuasion, *Good Road To Follow* is a more cross-genre offering than its immediate predecessors, co-written and co-produced by a variety of collaborators. OneRepublic's Ryan Tedder, steel guitar player Jerry Douglas, country and bluegrass veteran Jim Lauderdale: 'I got to step into the worlds of so many creative and inspiring people', Oates wrote on his website. 'Each song became an intense and focused creative experience'. It's the sound of a consummate player, at ease with himself and his position in the wider world; if Daryl Hall was experiencing the musicians he admired arriving on his doorstep for Daryl's internet show, Oates was finding a similar comradeship of musicians anxious to play with him, a continuing personal validation of his place.

Arkansas (2018)

His most recent studio album to date, *Arkansas*, clocks in at a light 34-minutes, recorded in Nashville and played by his Good Road Band; he described it as 'Dixieland dipped in bluegrass and salted with Delta Blues' and noted its gestation as a tribute to his beloved Mississippi John Hurt. Largely new interpretations of songs that have meant a lot to him across the years, he's not afraid to deploy that notion he has of the melody being the key part to be preserved in a cover version, with the arrangement, chord changes, feel and groove being 'up for grabs'. From this approach, Hurt's 'Make Me A Pallet On Your Floor' becomes his own 'Pallet Soft And Low' and a new reading is made of Hurt's 'My Creole Bell'. His voice has aged like a good whisky; this record never outstays its welcome and is a particularly strong summing up of John Oates as a musician and as a custodian of music from the past.

It Started With A Disc: Along The Red Ledge
(Originally published in *R2* / *Rock 'N' Reel* magazine)

It's hard to remember now, in these days where the entire stretch of musical history is accessible and acceptable. But there was a time when the narrow confines of genre made other styles off-limits and unapproachable. Punk was to blame, of course. When I was first buying singles back in 1977, you could buy reggae alongside the latest offering from The Clash, and it was okay to add a Motorhead to your haul of Damned LPs. If you were really switched on, you could acquire some Can, but peer pressure meant you really didn't want to step outside the boundaries too much. Amongst my very first haul of singles was 'Magic Fly' by French electro-disco band Space. God knows what my contemporaries thought.

There comes a time, though when you can see through social obstacles, and embrace a broader spectrum of listening. I remember hearing Daryl Hall and John Oates' 'I Can't Go For That (No Can Do)' at Newquay's Tall Trees nightclub in 1981 and instantly being attracted to the soulful power-pop that was their UK breakthrough album *Private Eyes*. And there's a certain joy in coming across an established act with a sizeable history behind them; having the opportunity to go backwards through their archive and see how they arrived at your own jumping-on point.

The Hall and Oates back-catalogue took me through their early folk-influenced demos, the Philadelphia soul of 'She's Gone' from *Abandoned Luncheonette*, to the soft-rock of the Todd-Rundgren-produced *War Babies*. It produced two should-have-been-huge pop/soul hybrids: the eponymous LP subsequently known as the 'silver' album, and the joyous *Bigger Than Both Of Us*. Then it spawned a stodgy rock album that Hall and Oates themselves despaired of: *Beauty On A Back Street*. 'I can't live with your totalitarian standards', Hall sang on one number in a less-than-slick lyric.

They bounced back, though, with the neglected gem that nestles in the middle of their most prolific years. Between March and April 1978, in Los Angeles, they cut *Along The Red Ledge* – according to biographer Nick Tosches, the LP they'd come to think of as their most overlooked work. My original copy was scored in Redruth's much-missed John Oliver's record shop during a hot summer filled with Atlantic surf, Cornish beaches and Newquay nightlife; the cassette player of my car resonating to a tape cut from this vinyl. I'd firmly stepped outside of my self-imposed musical confines.

It's not that it's a 'sun, sea and sand' LP though, it just caught that moment of casting off the shackles of punk devotion and breathing in fresher air. The songs themselves are ruminations on the passing of relationships and love affairs; little snapshots of times when you yearned in vain for things to continue or had flashes of realisation that affections were irrevocably dying. In that respect, it talked to someone just approaching adulthood, in that time frame where every new bond is alive and vital, and each split more gut-wrenching than the last. 'It's A Laugh', opening the record with Charlie DeChant's bittersweet saxophone, is Hall's sardonic reflection on a relationship – thought by 'everyone' to be 'forever' – now twisted and broken, yet it segues into Oates' gently-reflective 'Melody For A Memory'. So life goes.

The entire first side is taken up with these fractured situations; cathartic outpourings about drifting apart. George Harrison pops up to play guitar on 'The Last Time': regretful musings on a final parting that's far from desired by the song's narrator. They cut loose a little as the album goes on, sometimes to the detriment of the mood they'd previously established, particularly on the last track actually laid-down – 'Alley Katz' – which feels like a last-minute filler, and also with 'Serious Music': Oates' critique of 'sound but no electricity'. But they pull it back around on the unrestrained fun of 'Pleasure Beach', before spinning the album's overarching themes on its head with 'August Day'.

'August Day' – the LP's final track – is also its emotional heart: dark, melancholic and yet underpinned with optimism; Hall's music given sparse arrangement, adding to the humid oppression of long-time co-writer and then partner Sara Allen's brooding lyrics. Its resonance is in that moment of tightly-coiled waiting before the storm... 'Stir the dust and carve a rhyme,' it urges, conjuring images of thunder after a heat-filled day. 'I saw the sun, though it didn't shine', Allen writes, describing a 'sky colored heavy gray' and simply noting 'August day', leading into that most energizing event of all: taking a chance and saying 'I love you'. It's uncomplicated and underplayed, yet I get something from this song on every revisit.

I caught them at their peak. They seemed to slide gently downhill after *Private Eyes*, though its follow-up *H2O* spawned the AOR giant 'Maneater' and the deliciously sensual 'One On One'. And it's a cliché, but true to highlight their performance on the US-leg of Live Aid as that day's stateside high point. I completely lost touch with their work after 1988's patchy *Ooh Yeah!*, though it had its moments – such as the sharply-observed acclamation of city-living 'Downtown Life', when they take a withering look at 'Yuppies in black doing white-collar crime', who, in their eyes, 'scared away the local color'.

The Japanese CD of *Along The Red Ledge* that I picked up in Tower Records, Piccadilly Circus, sometime around 1989 however, still gets pulled out when the air hangs heavy with approaching summer storms, and 'August Day' reflects and elaborates the mood.

Resources and Further Reading
Books
Oates, J., Epting, C., *Change Of Seasons: A Memoir* (St Martin's Press, 2017)
Tosches, N., *Dangerous Dances* (Sidgwick & Jackson, 1985)

Internet
HallandOates.com
Facebook: Hall & Oates: No Goodbyes
Hallandoates.de: German website, not recently updated but with magazine scans and gig lists
Forums.SteveHoffman.tv: lively and knowledgeable archived message board
Rocksbackpages.com
Treblezine.com: Paul Pearson's excellent overview *'Celebrate the Catalogue: Hall & Oates'*
Chrisepting.com: Co-author of John Oates' *Change Of Seasons: A Memoir*
Kamertunesblog.wordpress.com: Rich Kamerman's well-considered H&O albums survey

Also available from Sonicbond Publishing

On Track series

Tori Amos – Lisa Torem 978-1-78952-142-9
Asia – Peter Braidis 978-1-78952-099-6
Barclay James Harvest – Keith and Monica Domone 978-1-78952-067-5
The Beatles – Andrew Wild 978-1-78952-009-5
The Beatles Solo 1969-1980 – Andrew Wild 978-1-78952-030-9
Blue Oyster Cult – Jacob Holm-Lupo 978-1-78952-007-1
Marc Bolan and T.Rex – Peter Gallagher 978-1-78952-124-5
Kate Bush – Bill Thomas 978-1-78952-097-2
Camel – Hamish Kuzminski 978-1-78952-040-8
Caravan – Andy Boot 978-1-78952-127-6
Cardiacs – Eric Benac 978-1-78952-131-3
Eric Clapton Solo – Andrew Wild 978-1-78952-141-2
The Clash – Nick Assirati 978-1-78952-077-4
Crosby, Stills and Nash – Andrew Wild 978-1-78952-039-2
The Damned – Morgan Brown 978-1-78952-136-8
Deep Purple and Rainbow 1968-79 – Steve Pilkington 978-1-78952-002-6
Dire Straits – Andrew Wild 978-1-78952-044-6
The Doors – Tony Thompson 978-1-78952-137-5
Dream Theater – Jordan Blum 978-1-78952-050-7
Elvis Costello and The Attractions – Georg Purvis 978-1-78952-129-0
Emerson Lake and Palmer – Mike Goode 978-1-78952-000-2
Fairport Convention – Kevan Furbank 978-1-78952-051-4
Peter Gabriel – Graeme Scarfe 978-1-78952-138-2
Genesis – Stuart MacFarlane 978-1-78952-005-7
Gentle Giant – Gary Steel 978-1-78952-058-3
Gong – Kevan Furbank 978-1-78952-082-8
Hawkwind – Duncan Harris 978-1-78952-052-1
Roy Harper – Opher Goodwin 978-1-78952-130-6
Iron Maiden – Steve Pilkington 978-1-78952-061-3
Jefferson Airplane – Richard Butterworth 978-1-78952-143-6
Jethro Tull – Jordan Blum 978-1-78952-016-3
Elton John in the 1970s – Peter Kearns 978-1-78952-034-7
The Incredible String Band – Tim Moon 978-1-78952-107-8
Iron Maiden – Steve Pilkington 978-1-78952-061-3
Judas Priest – John Tucker 978-1-78952-018-7
Kansas – Kevin Cummings 978-1-78952-057-6
Led Zeppelin – Steve Pilkington 978-1-78952-151-1

Level 42 – Matt Philips 978-1-78952-102-3
Aimee Mann – Jez Rowden 978-1-78952-036-1
Joni Mitchell – Peter Kearns 978-1-78952-081-1
The Moody Blues – Geoffrey Feakes 978-1-78952-042-2
Mike Oldfield – Ryan Yard 978-1-78952-060-6
Tom Petty – Richard James 978-1-78952-128-3
Porcupine Tree – Nick Holmes 978-1-78952-144-3
Queen – Andrew Wild 978-1-78952-003-3
Radiohead – William Allen 978-1-78952-149-8
Renaissance – David Detmer 978-1-78952-062-0
The Rolling Stones 1963-80 – Steve Pilkington 978-1-78952-017-0
The Smiths and Morrissey – Tommy Gunnarsson 978-1-78952-140-5
Steely Dan – Jez Rowden 978-1-78952-043-9
Steve Hackett – Geoffrey Feakes 978-1-78952-098-9
Thin Lizzy – Graeme Stroud 978-1-78952-064-4
Toto – Jacob Holm-Lupo 978-1-78952-019-4
U2 – Eoghan Lyng 978-1-78952-078-1
UFO – Richard James 978-1-78952-073-6
The Who – Geoffrey Feakes 978-1-78952-076-7
Roy Wood and the Move – James R Turner 978-1-78952-008-8
Van Der Graaf Generator – Dan Coffey 978-1-78952-031-6
Yes – Stephen Lambe 978-1-78952-001-9
Frank Zappa 1966 to 1979 – Eric Benac 978-1-78952-033-0
10CC – Peter Kearns 978-1-78952-054-5

Decades Series
The Bee Gees in the 1960s – Andrew Mon Hughes et al
978-1-78952-148-1
Alice Cooper in the 1970s – Chris Sutton 978-1-78952-104-7
Curved Air in the 1970s – Laura Shenton 978-1-78952-069-9
Fleetwood Mac in the 1970s – Andrew Wild 978-1-78952-105-4
Focus in the 1970s – Stephen Lambe 978-1-78952-079-8
Genesis in the 1970s – Bill Thomas 978178952-146-7
Marillion in the 1980s – Nathaniel Webb 978-1-78952-065-1
Pink Floyd In The 1970s – Georg Purvis 978-1-78952-072-9
The Sweet in the 1970s – Darren Johnson 978-1-78952-139-9
Uriah Heep in the 1970s – Steve Pilkington 978-1-78952-103-0
Yes in the 1980s – Stephen Lambe with David Watkinson
978-1-78952-125-2

On Screen series

Carry On... – Stephen Lambe 978-1-78952-004-0

David Cronenberg – Patrick Chapman 978-1-78952-071-2

Doctor Who: The David Tennant Years –
Jamie Hailstone 978-1-78952-066-8

Monty Python – Steve Pilkington 978-1-78952-047-7

Seinfeld Seasons 1 to 5 – Stephen Lambe 978-1-78952-012-5

James Bond – Andrew Wild 978-1-78952-010-1

Other Books

Babysitting A Band On The Rocks – G.D. Praetorius 978-1-78952-106-1

Derek Taylor: For Your Radioactive Children –
Andrew Darlington 978-1-78952-038-5

Iggy and The Stooges On Stage 1967-1974 – Per Nilsen 978-1-78952-101-6

Jon Anderson and the Warriors – the road to Yes –
David Watkinson 978-1-78952-059-0

Nu Metal: A Definitive Guide – Matt Karpe 978-1-78952-063-7

Tommy Bolin: In and Out of Deep Purple – Laura Shenton 978-1-78952-070-5

Maximum Darkness – Deke Leonard 978-1-78952-048-4

Maybe I Should've Stayed In Bed – Deke Leonard 978-1-78952-053-8

Psychedelic Rock in 1967 – Kevan Furbank 978-1-78952-155-9

The Twang Dynasty – Deke Leonard 978-1-78952-049-1

and many more to come!

Would you like to write for Sonicbond Publishing?

We are mainly a music publisher, but we also occasionally publish in other genres including film and television. At Sonicbond Publishing we are always on the look-out for authors, particularly for our two main series, On Track and Decades.

Mixing fact with in depth analysis, the On Track series examines the entire recorded work of a particular musical artist or group. All genres are considered from easy listening and jazz to 60s soul to 90s pop, via rock and metal.

The Decades series singles out a particular decade in an artist or group's history and focuses on that decade in more detail than may be allowed in the On Track series.

While professional writing experience would, of course, be an advantage, the most important qualification is to have real enthusiasm and knowledge of your subject. First-time authors are welcomed, but the ability to write well in English is essential.

Sonicbond Publishing has distribution throughout Europe and North America, and all our books are also published in E-book form. Authors will be paid a royalty based on sales of their book. Further details about our books are available from www.sonicbondpublishing.com. To contact us, complete the contact form there or email info@sonicbondpublishing.co.uk